OPPOSING VIEWPOINTS® SERIES

Gender Roles

Other Books of Related Interest

Opposing Viewpoints Series
Civil Liberties
The Culture of Beauty
Gay Parenting
Gendercide

At Issue Series
Are Women Paid Fairly?
Beauty Pageants

Current Controversies Series
Military Families
The Wage Gap
Women in Politics

"Congress shall make no law . . . abridging the freedom of speech, or of the press."

First Amendment to the US Constitution

The basic foundation of our democracy is the First Amendment guarantee of freedom of expression. The Opposing Viewpoints Series is dedicated to the concept of this basic freedom and the idea that it is more important to practice it than to enshrine it.

Gender Roles

Noël Merino, Book Editor

GREENHAVEN PRESS
A part of Gale, Cengage Learning

GALE
CENGAGE Learning·

Farmington Hills, Mich • San Francisco • New York • Waterville, Maine
Meriden, Conn • Mason, Ohio • Chicago

Elizabeth Des Chenes, *Director, Content Strategy*
Cynthia Sanner, *Publisher*
Douglas Dentino, *Manager, New Product*

© 2014 Greenhaven Press, a part of Gale, Cengage Learning.

WCN: 01-100-101

Gale and Greenhaven Press are registered trademarks used herein under license.

For more information, contact:
Greenhaven Press
27500 Drake Rd.
Farmington Hills, MI 48331-3535
Or you can visit our Internet site at gale.cengage.com

For product information and technology assistance, contact us at

Gale Customer Support, 1-800-877-4253
For permission to use material from this text or product, submit all requests online at
www.cengage.com/permissions

Further permissions questions can be emailed to permissionrequest@cengage.com

Articles in Greenhaven Press anthologies are often edited for length to meet page requirements. In addition, original titles of these works are changed to clearly present the main thesis and to explicitly indicate the author's opinion. Every effort is made to ensure that Greenhaven Press accurately reflects the original intent of the authors. Every effort has been made to trace the owners of copyrighted material.

Cover image copyright © Cameron Whitman/Shutterstock.com.

LIBRARY OF CONGRESS CATALOGING-IN-PUBLICATION DATA

Gender roles / edited by Noël Merino, book editor.
    pages cm. -- (Opposing viewpoints)
    Includes bibliographical references and index.
    ISBN 978-0-7377-6957-9 (hardcover) -- ISBN 978-0-7377-6958-6 (paperback)
    1. Sex role. I. Merino, Noël, editor of compilation.
    HQ1075.G4663 2014
    305.3--dc23
                                                        2013049848

Printed in the United States of America
1 2 3 4 5 6 7 18 17 16 15 14

Contents

Chapter 3: How Do Gender Roles Affect the Workplace?

Chapter 4: How Are Gender Roles Changing?

Why Consider
Opposing Viewpoints?

> *"The only way in which a human being can make some approach to knowing the whole of a subject is by hearing what can be said about it by persons of every variety of opinion and studying all modes in which it can be looked at by every character of mind. No wise man ever acquired his wisdom in any mode but this."*
>
> *John Stuart Mill*

In our media-intensive culture it is not difficult to find differing opinions. Thousands of newspapers and magazines and dozens of radio and television talk shows resound with differing points of view. The difficulty lies in deciding which opinion to agree with and which "experts" seem the most credible. The more inundated we become with differing opinions and claims, the more essential it is to hone critical reading and thinking skills to evaluate these ideas. Opposing Viewpoints books address this problem directly by presenting stimulating debates that can be used to enhance and teach these skills. The varied opinions contained in each book examine many different aspects of a single issue. While examining these conveniently edited opposing views, readers can develop critical thinking skills such as the ability to compare and contrast authors' credibility, facts, argumentation styles, use of persuasive techniques, and other stylistic tools. In short, the Opposing Viewpoints Series is an ideal way to attain the higher-level thinking and reading skills so essential in a culture of diverse and contradictory opinions.

In addition to providing a tool for critical thinking, Opposing Viewpoints books challenge readers to question their own strongly held opinions and assumptions. Most people form their opinions on the basis of upbringing, peer pressure, and personal, cultural, or professional bias. By reading carefully balanced opposing views, readers must directly confront new ideas as well as the opinions of those with whom they disagree. This is not to simplistically argue that everyone who reads opposing views will—or should—change his or her opinion. Instead, the series enhances readers' understanding of their own views by encouraging confrontation with opposing ideas. Careful examination of others' views can lead to the readers' understanding of the logical inconsistencies in their own opinions, perspective on why they hold an opinion, and the consideration of the possibility that their opinion requires further evaluation.

Evaluating Other Opinions

To ensure that this type of examination occurs, Opposing Viewpoints books present all types of opinions. Prominent spokespeople on different sides of each issue as well as well-known professionals from many disciplines challenge the reader. An additional goal of the series is to provide a forum for other, less known, or even unpopular viewpoints. The opinion of an ordinary person who has had to make the decision to cut off life support from a terminally ill relative, for example, may be just as valuable and provide just as much insight as a medical ethicist's professional opinion. The editors have two additional purposes in including these less known views. One, the editors encourage readers to respect others' opinions—even when not enhanced by professional credibility. It is only by reading or listening to and objectively evaluating others' ideas that one can determine whether they are worthy of consideration. Two, the inclusion of such viewpoints encourages the important critical thinking skill of objectively evaluating an author's credentials and bias. This evaluation will illuminate an author's reasons for taking a particular stance on an issue and will aid in readers' evaluation of the author's ideas.

It is our hope that these books will give readers a deeper understanding of the issues debated and an appreciation of the complexity of even seemingly simple issues when good and honest people disagree. This awareness is particularly important in a democratic society such as ours in which people enter into public debate to determine the common good. Those with whom one disagrees should not be regarded as enemies but rather as people whose views deserve careful examination and may shed light on one's own.

Thomas Jefferson once said that "difference of opinion leads to inquiry, and inquiry to truth." Jefferson, a broadly educated man, argued that "if a nation expects to be ignorant and free . . . it expects what never was and never will be." As individuals and as a nation, it is imperative that we consider the opinions of others and examine them with skill and discernment. The Opposing Viewpoints Series is intended to help readers achieve this goal.

David L. Bender and Bruno Leone,
Founders

Introduction

> *"The term* gender role *is used to signify all those things that a person says or does to disclose himself or herself as having the status of boy or man, girl or woman, respectively. It includes, but is not restricted to, sexuality in the sense of eroticism."*
>
> —*John Money,*
> *psychologist and sexologist,*
> *1921–2006*

In 1955, psychologist and sexologist John Money first coined the term 'gender role.' He developed the term to differentiate the behaviors and actions of a person from that individual's biological or assigned sex. Money's research identified a distinction between behaviors related to one's biological sex (determined by a combination of external sex organs, chromosomes, and hormones) and those related to social practices and individual gender identity. Money did not deny that there are physical differences between men and women, but he did distinguish these physical differences from the behaviors people engage in that could be deemed as masculine or feminine. Furthermore, Money's research on hermaphroditism (the occurrence of both male and female sexual organs in one person) noted the problems with a binary, or dual, theory of biological sex and posited that culturally assigned sex was more important to future gender identity and gender role behavior.

Physical differences do exist between biological males and biological females. The very criteria for determining biological sex illustrate differences in reproductive organs, genetics, and hormones (and also illustrate the problem with using only two categories, since these three criteria do not always result in a clear categorization of "male" or "female"). Brain research has shown that female brains are stronger in the regions that rule language, whereas male brains are stronger in the regions associated with visual perception, tracking objects through space, and form recognition. Nonetheless, the research on differences draws conclusions for men and women *on average*, which means that for any particular man and woman, it may not be the case that the man has higher form recognition or that the woman has better language skills.

In contrast to physical sex differences, gender roles are sets of behaviors and actions associated with men and women, what might be deemed as masculine or feminine. In 1955, Money, along with psychologists Joan Hampson and John Hampson, detailed examples of behaviors and actions that constitute one's gender role:

> Gender role is appraised in relation to the following: general mannerisms, deportment and demeanor; spontaneous topics of talk in unprompted conversation and casual comment; content of dreams, daydreams and fantasies; replies to oblique inquiries and projective tests; evidence of erotic practices and, finally, the person's replies to direct inquiry.

Whereas sex is associated with relatively fixed physical differences, gender roles are related to ongoing behaviors and actions.

To what extent gender roles are a natural result of biological sex is debatable. On the one end of the spectrum are those who believe that gender roles are imposed from without, through a variety of social influences. In 1973 noted French philosopher Simone de Beauvoir wrote, "One is not born a woman, but, rather, becomes one." On this view, social norms transferred by parents, peers, and teachers influence people into behaving in ways that are sex appropriate. These behaviors constitute the gender role that one takes on from an early age. On the other end of the spectrum are those who argue that real physiological differences explain some or all of the affinities seen in gender roles. Biopsychologists have undertaken research that connects biological sex with gender behavior. For instance, social psychologist James M. Dabbs Jr., along with other researchers, claims to have found a link between testosterone and aggression. According to the first view above, which denies a connection between biological sex and gender, men learn to express themselves through aggression and violence. On the second view, there is a biological basis for this masculine behavior.

It is clear that gender roles exist, but whether they are necessary or fixed in some manner is open to debate. *Opposing Viewpoints: Gender Roles* explores the relevance of and changing nature of the roles played by males and females in four chapters, which are titled: Are Gender Roles Important?, How Do Gender Roles Affect Parenting and Reproduction?, How Do Gender Roles Affect the Workplace?, and How Are Gender Roles Changing? The various viewpoints explored in these chapters illustrate the wide divergence of opinion on the biological basis of gender roles and the extent to which expectations of gender roles are beneficial or harmful.

OPPOSING
VIEWPOINTS®
SERIES

CHAPTER 1

Are Gender Roles Important?

Chapter Preface

Many of the debates about subverting traditional gender roles hinge on whether or not traditional gender roles are beneficial. Those wanting to preserve traditional roles frequently make the case that the roles exist because they lead to a better, or more natural, arrangement of society and institutions. Those wanting to eliminate traditional gender roles often believe that such roles are not only arbitrary but also limiting and even potentially damaging. A recent controversy illustrates these competing views.

US Army soldier Bradley Manning became well known to the American public through his trial and conviction for violations of the Espionage Act. His release of classified information caused much controversy; but after his sentencing in August 2013 he caused a new public controversy by announcing his gender change:

> As I transition into this next phase of my life, I want everyone to know the real me. I am Chelsea Manning. I am a female. Given the way that I feel, and have felt since childhood, I want to begin hormone therapy as soon as possible. I hope that you will support me in this transition. I also request that, starting today, you refer to me by my new name and use the feminine pronoun (except in official mail to the confinement facility).

Having lived as a gendered male for twenty-five years, Chelsea Manning's announcement was a source of public curiosity, with both outrage and support expressed.

National Review correspondent Kevin D. Williamson says, "We have created a rhetoric of 'gender identity' that is disconnected from biological sexual fact." He claims that language is part of the problem:

It is not an accident that a literary term received the promotion over a scientific one: "Gender" overtook "sex" linguistically at the same time that "gender," which denotes male-female differences that are, in the debased language of the time, "socially constructed," overtook "sex," which denotes male-female differences that are biological, as a guiding consideration. Every battle in the war on reality begins with the opening of a new linguistic front.

Williamson believes that the desire for gender reassignment is a kind of illness, not a legitimate choice.

Writer Kathleen Geier argues that transgender people should be treated in the way that they prefer, "including referring to transgender people by the names and pronouns they prefer. She says, "A shocking 41 percent of transgender Americans have attempted suicide, and transgender people, especially transgender women of color, are disproportionately targeted for hate crimes." *Reason* associate editor Scott Shackford argues that the gender identity of Chelsea Manning is really nobody's business: "The bigger question is 'Why should it matter to any of us if Bradley Manning becomes Chelsea Manning?' Why should there be resistance to referring to Chelsea as a woman? What does it mean to any of us at all if Manning puts on a blond wig and starts taking hormones?"

The reaction to Chelsea Manning's announcement depends a great deal on how important one believes traditional gender roles are. As authors in this chapter illustrate, current controversies about issues such as same-sex marriage and gender neutrality in the military depend on views about the significance of gender roles. If traditional gender roles reflect good social arrangements, then there is an argument for keeping things as they have been. If they do not necessarily lead to social good, then the argument can be made for dismantling or rearranging the passé tradition.

| *"Sex differences have at least some foundation in biology."*

Gender Preferences Are Connected to Biological Sex from an Early Age

Christina Hoff Sommers

In the following viewpoint, Christina Hoff Sommers argues that attempts to eliminate gender roles, as in Swedish classrooms, are intolerant and bound to fail. Sommers claims that there is evidence that biology is behind many of the sex-typed behaviors seen in men and women. Furthermore, she contends that researchers have found benefits to gendered play in childhood. She concludes that gender roles are not something to be fixed or eliminated but, rather, to be accepted. Sommers is a resident scholar at the American Enterprise Institute and author of The War Against Boys: How Misguided Policies Are Harming Our Young Men.

As you read, consider the following questions:

1. According to Sommers, Top-Toy introduced gender neutrality in its catalog by doing what?

2. Girls with congenital adrenal hyperplasia prefer what kind of toys, as stated by the author?

3. Sommers draws an analogy between the way Swedes are treating gender-conforming children to the way who was once treated?

Is it discriminatory and degrading for toy catalogs to show girls playing with tea sets and boys with Nerf guns? A Swedish regulatory group says yes. The Reklamombudsmannen (RO) has reprimanded Top-Toy, a licensee of Toys"R"Us and one of the largest toy companies in Northern Europe, for its "outdated" advertisements and has pressured it to mend its "narrow-minded" ways. After receiving "training and guidance" from RO equity experts, Top-Toy introduced gender neutrality in its 2012 Christmas catalog. The catalog shows little boys playing with a Barbie Dream House and girls with guns and gory action figures. As its marketing director explains, "For several years, we have found that the gender debate has grown so strong in the Swedish market that we have had to adjust."

The Male and Female Distinction

Swedes can be remarkably thorough in their pursuit of gender parity. A few years ago, a feminist political party proposed a law requiring men to sit while urinating—less messy and more equal. In 2004, the leader of Sweden's Left Party Feminist Council, Gudrun Schyman, proposed a "man tax"—a special tariff to be levied on men to pay for all the violence and mayhem wrought by their sex. In April 2012, following the celebration of International Women's Day, the Swedes formally introduced the genderless pronoun "hen" to be used in place of he and she (han and hon).

Egalia, a new state-sponsored pre-school in Stockholm, is dedicated to the total obliteration of the male and female distinction. There are no boys and girls at Egalia—just "friends" and "buddies." Classic fairy tales like *Cinderella* and *Snow White* have been replaced by tales of two male giraffes who parent abandoned crocodile eggs. The Swedish Green Party would like Egalia to be the norm: It has suggested placing gender watchdogs in all of the nation's preschools. "Egalia gives [children] a fantastic opportunity to be whoever they want to be," says one excited teacher. (It is probably necessary to add that this is not an Orwellian satire or a right-wing fantasy: This school actually exists.)

The problem with Egalia and gender-neutral toy catalogs is that boys and girls, on average, do not have identical interests, propensities, or needs. Twenty years ago, Hasbro, a major American toy manufacturing company, tested a playhouse it hoped to market to both boys and girls. It soon emerged that girls and boys did not interact with the structure in the same way. The girls dressed the dolls, kissed them, and played house. The boys catapulted the toy baby carriage from the roof. A Hasbro manager came up with a novel explanation: "Boys and girls are different."

They are different, and nothing short of radical and sustained behavior modification could significantly change their elemental play preferences. Children, with few exceptions, are powerfully drawn to sex-stereotyped play. David Geary, a developmental psychologist at the University of Missouri, told me in an email, "One of the largest and most persistent differences between the sexes are children's play preferences." The female preference for nurturing play and the male propensity for rough-and-tumble hold cross-culturally and even cross-species (with a few exceptions—female spotted hyenas seem to be at least as aggressive as males). Among our close relatives such as vervet and rhesus monkeys, researchers have found that females play with dolls far more than their brothers, who prefer balls and toy cars. It seems unlikely that the monkeys were indoctrinated by stereotypes in a Top-Toy catalog. Something else is going on.

The Role of Biology

Biology appears to play a role. Several animal studies have shown that hormonal manipulation can reverse sex-typed behavior. When researchers exposed female rhesus monkeys to male hormones prenatally, these females later displayed male-like levels of rough-and-tumble play. Similar results are found in human beings. Congenital adrenal hyperplasia (CAH) is a genetic condition that results when the female fetus is subjected to unusually large quantities of male hormones—adrenal androgens. Girls with CAH tend to prefer trucks, cars, and construction sets over dolls and play tea sets. As psychologist Doreen Kimura reported in *Scientific American*, "These findings suggest that these preferences were actually altered in some way by the early hormonal environment." They also cast doubt on the view that gender-specific play is primarily shaped by socialization.

Professor Geary does not have much hope for the new gender-blind toy catalog: "The catalog will almost certainly disappear in a few years, once parents who buy from it realize their kids don't want these toys." Most little girls don't want to play with dump trucks, as almost any parent can attest. Including me: When my granddaughter Eliza was given a toy train, she placed it in a baby carriage and covered it with a blanket so it could get some sleep.

Androgyny advocates like our Swedish friends have heard such stories many times, and they have an answer. They acknowledge that sex differences have at least some foundation in biology, but they insist that culture can intensify or diminish their power and effect. Even if Eliza is prompted by nature to interact with a train in a stereotypical female way, that is no reason for her parents not to energetically correct her. Hunter College psychologist Virginia Valian, a strong proponent of Swedish-style re-genderization, wrote in the book *Why So Slow? The Advancement of Women*, "We do not accept biology as destiny . . . We vaccinate, we inoculate, we medicate. . . I propose we adopt the same attitude toward biological sex differences."

Valian is absolutely right that we do not have to accept biology as destiny. But the analogy is ludicrous: We vaccinate, inoculate, and medicate children against *disease*. Is being a gender-typical little boy or girl a pathology in need of a cure? Failure to protect children from small pox, diphtheria, or measles places them in harm's way. I don't believe there is any such harm in allowing male/female differences to flourish in early childhood. As one Swedish mother, Tanja Bergkvist, told the Associated Press, "Different gender roles aren't problematic as long as they are equally valued." Gender neutrality is not a necessary condition for equality. Men and women can be different—but equal. And for most human beings, the differences are a vital source for meaning and happiness. Since when is uniformity a democratic ideal?

The Healthy Development of Children

Few would deny that parents and teachers should expose children to a wide range of toys and play activities. But what the Swedes are now doing in some of their classrooms goes far beyond encouraging children to experiment with different toys and play styles—they are *requiring* it. And toy companies who resist the gender neutrality mandate face official censure. Is this kind of social engineering worth it? Is it even ethical?

To succeed, the Swedish parents, teachers and authorities are going to have to police—incessantly—boys' powerful attraction to large-group rough-and-tumble play and girls' affinity for intimate theatrical play. As Geary says, "You can change some of these behaviors with reinforcement and monitoring, but they bounce back once this stops." But this constant monitoring can also undermine children's healthy development.

Anthony Pellegrini, a professor of early childhood education at the University of Minnesota, defines the kind of rough-and-tumble play that boys favor as a behavior that includes "laughing, running, smiling, jumping, open-hand beating, wrestling, play fighting, chasing and fleeing." This kind of play is often mistakenly regarded as aggression, but according to Pellegrini, it is the very opposite. In cases of schoolyard aggression, the participants are unhappy, they part as enemies, and there are often tears and injuries. Rough-and-tumble play brings boys together, makes them happy, and is a critical part of their social development.

Researchers Mary Ellin Logue (University of Maine) and Hattie Harvey (University of Denver) agree, and they have documented the benefits of boys' "bad guy" superhero action narratives. Teachers tend not to like such play, say Logue and Harvey, but it improves boys' conversation, creative writing skills, and moral imagination. Swedish boys, like American boys, are languishing far behind girls in school. In a 2009 study Logue and Harvey ask an important question the Swedes should consider: "If boys, due to their choices of dramatic play themes, are discouraged from dramatic play, how will this affect their early language and literacy development and their engagement in school?"

What about the girls? Nearly 30 years ago, Vivian Gussin Paley, a beloved kindergarten teacher at the Chicago Laboratory Schools and winner of a MacArthur "genius" award, published a classic book on children's play entitled *Boys & Girls: Superheroes in the Doll Corner*. Paley wondered if girls are missing out by not partaking in boys' superhero play, but her observations of the "doll corner" allayed her doubts. Girls, she learned, are interested in their own kind of domination. Boys' imaginative play involves a lot of conflict and imaginary violence; girls' play, on the other hand, seems to be much gentler and more peaceful. But as Paley looked more carefully, she noticed that the girls' fantasies were just as exciting and in-

The Evolution of Male and Female Brains

To understand human behavior—how men and women differ from one another, for instance—we must look beyond the demands of modern life. Our brains are essentially like those of our ancestors of 50,000 and more years ago, and we can gain some insight into sex differences by studying the differing roles men and women have played in evolutionary history. Men were responsible for hunting and scavenging, defending the group against predators and enemies, and shaping and using weapons. Women gathered food near the home base, tended the home, prepared food and clothing, and cared for small children. Such specialization would put different selection pressures on men and women.

Doreen Kimura,
Scientific American, *May 2002.*

tense as the boys—though different. They were full of conflict, pesky characters and imaginary power struggles. "Mothers and princesses are as powerful as any superheroes the boys can devise." Paley appreciated the benefits of gendered play for both sexes, and she had no illusions about the prospects for its elimination: "Kindergarten is a triumph of sexual self-stereotyping. No amount of adult subterfuge or propaganda deflects the five-year-old's passion for segregation by sex."

But subterfuge and propaganda appear to be the order of the day in Sweden. In their efforts to free children from the constraints of gender, the Swedish reformers are imposing their own set of inviolate rules, standards, and taboos. Here is how *Slate* author Nathalie Rothchild describes a gender-neutral classroom:

One Swedish school got rid of its toy cars because boys "gender-coded" them and ascribed the cars higher status than other toys. Another preschool removed "free playtime" from its schedule because, as a pedagogue at the school put it, when children play freely 'stereotypical gender patterns are born and cemented. In free play there is hierarchy, exclusion, and the seed to bullying.' And so every detail of children's interactions gets micromanaged by concerned adults, who end up problematizing minute aspects of children's lives, from how they form friendships to what games they play and what songs they sing.

The Swedes are treating gender-conforming children the way we once treated gender-variant children. Formerly called "tomboy girls" and "sissy boys" in the medical literature, these kids are persistently attracted to the toys of the opposite sex. They will often remain fixated on the "wrong" toys despite relentless, often cruel pressure from parents, doctors, and peers. Their total immersion in sex-stereotyped culture—a non-stop Toys"R"Us indoctrination—seems to have little effect on their passion for the toys of the opposite sex. There was a time when a boy who displayed a persistent aversion to trucks and rough play and a fixation on frilly dolls or princess paraphernalia would have been considered a candidate for behavior modification therapy. Today, most experts encourage tolerance, understanding, and acceptance: just leave him alone and let him play as he wants. The Swedes should extend the same tolerant understanding to the gender identity and preferences of the vast majority of children.

| "*Gender is not inherently nor solely connected to one's physical anatomy.*"

Gender Is Not Inherently Connected to Biology

Gender Spectrum

In the following viewpoint, the organization Gender Spectrum argues that accepted social gender roles are not tied to a person's sex. The organization claims that there is actually a wide variety of gender variance among people, regardless of biological sex, and that accepted gender roles in society have changed over time and vary across cultures. The Gender Spectrum claims that there ought to be more acceptance for people who do not assume typical gender roles. Gender Spectrum is an organization that provides education, training, and support to help create a gender-sensitive and inclusive environment for all children and teens.

As you read, consider the following questions:

1. How does the author define gender?

2. By age three most children exhibit typical gender behavior caused by what two things, according to Gender Spectrum?

"Understanding Gender," Gender Spectrum, 2009. www.genderspectrum.org. Copyright © 2009 by Gender Spectrum. All rights reserved. Reproduced by permission.

3. Which three cultures have a complex understanding of gender, according to the author?

For many people, the terms "gender" and "sex" are used interchangeably, and thus incorrectly. This idea has become so common, particularly in western societies, that it is rarely questioned. We are born, assigned a gender, and sent out into the world. For many people, this is cause for little, if any dissonance. Yet biological sex and gender are different; gender is not inherently nor solely connected to one's physical anatomy.

Biological Gender (sex) includes physical attributes such as external genitalia, sex chromosomes, gonads, sex hormones, and internal reproductive structures. At birth, it is used to assign sex; that is, to identify individuals as male or female. *Gender* on the other hand is far more complicated. It is the complex interrelationship between an individual's sex and one's internal sense of self as male, female, both or neither as well as one's outward presentations and behaviors related to that perception. Together the intersection of these three dimensions produces one's authentic sense of gender, both in how they experience their own gender as well as how others perceive it.

The Gender Spectrum

Western culture has come to view gender as a binary concept, with two rigidly fixed options: male or female. When a child is born, a quick glance between the legs determines the gender label that the child will carry for life. But even if gender is to be restricted to basic biology, a binary concept still fails to capture the rich variation observed. Rather than just two distinct boxes, biological gender occurs across a continuum of possibilities. This spectrum of anatomical variations by itself should be enough to disregard the simplistic notions of a binary gender system.

But beyond anatomy, there are multiple domains defining gender. In turn, these domains can be independently characterized across a range of possibilities. Instead of the static, binary model produced through a solely physical understanding of gender, a far richer tapestry of biology, gender expression, and gender identity intersect in a multidimensional array of possibilities. Quite simply, the gender spectrum represents a more nuanced, and ultimately truly authentic model of human gender.

Gender is all around us. Like water surrounding a fish, we are unaware of its ever-present nature. Gender is actually taught to us, from the moment we are born. Gender expectations and messages bombard us constantly. Upbringing, culture, peers, community, media, and religion, are some of the many influences that shape our understanding of this core aspect of self. How you learned and interacted with gender as a young child directly influences how you view the world today. Gendered interaction between parent and child begin as soon as the sex of the baby is known. In short, gender is a socially constructed concept.

Gender Variance

Like other social constructs, gender is closely monitored and reinforced by society. Practically everything in society is assigned a gender—toys, colors, clothes and behaviors are just some of the more obvious examples. Through a combination of social conditioning and personal preference, by age three most children prefer activities and exhibit behaviors typically associated with their sex. Accepted social gender roles and expectations are so entrenched in our culture that most people cannot imagine any other way. As a result, individuals fitting neatly into these expectations rarely if ever question what *gender* really means. They have never had to, because the system has worked for them.

Gender variance is when a person's preferences and self-expression fall outside commonly understood gender norms, or when one's internal gender identity does not align with the sex assigned at birth. Gender variance is a normal part of human experience, across cultures and throughout history. Nonbinary gender diversity exists all over the world, documented by countless historians and anthropologists. Examples of individuals living comfortably outside of typical male/female expectations and/or identities are found in every region of the globe. The *calabai*, and *calalai* of Indonesia, two-spirit Native Americans, and the *hijra* of India all represent more complex understandings of gender than allowed for by a simplistic binary model.

Further, what might be considered gender variant in one period of history may become gender normative in another. One need only examine trends related to men wearing earrings or women sporting tattoos to quickly see the malleability of social expectations about gender. Even the seemingly intractable "pink is for girls, blue is for boys" notions are relatively new. While there is some debate about the reasons why they reversed, what is well documented is that not until the mid-twentieth century were notions of pink for girls or blue for boys so firmly ensconced. You can make the case that "pink is the new blue!".

Gender and Privilege

When someone is "typically gendered (or cisgendered)," they benefit from gender privilege. For individuals whose biological sex, gender expression, and gender identity neatly align, there is a level of congruence as they encounter the world. Like many forms of social privilege, this is frequently an unexamined aspect of their lives. Forms they fill out, the clothing stores in which they shop, or identification papers they carry bring few if any second thoughts. Yet for a transgender or gender nonconforming person, each of these, and many more examples, are constant reminders that they move about in a culture that really does not account for their own experience. Social privilege comes from an assumption that one's own perspective is universal; whether related to race, or language, or gender, privilege comes from being part of the "norm." Or, as Dorothy Soelle aptly described it: *Privilege is being able to choose what you will not see.*

To understand this more intuitively, think about the last time you were in a public setting and needed to use a restroom. For cisgender individuals, this rarely presents a problem or question (issues of cleanliness notwithstanding!). Yet for an individual who does not fit into narrowly defined expectations of gender presentation or identity, restroom use can present a whole host of challenges, sometimes even becoming a matter of life and death. The daily need to make judgments about what one does, or wears, or says based on other people's perceptions of their gender is a burden that many people never encounter. These everyday reminders of being different are also constant reinforcement of being "other."

Greater Acceptance for All

Perhaps the most fundamental aspect of a person's identity, gender deeply influences every part of one's life. In a society where this crucial aspect of self has been so narrowly defined and rigidly enforced, individuals who exists outside its norms face innumerable challenges. Even those who vary only slightly from the norm can become targets of disapproval. Yet this does not have to be the case for ever. Through a thoughtful consideration of the uniqueness and validity of every person's experiences of self, we can develop greater acceptance for all. Not only will this create greater inclusion for individuals who challenge the norms of gender, it will actually create space for all individuals to more fully explore and celebrate who they are.

*"These aspects of marriage—the comple-
mentarity of male and female, and the
irreplaceable role of male-female relations in reproducing the human race—
are part of the original order of creation."*

Marriage Is Meant to Be the Union of One Man and One Woman

Andreas J. Köstenberger

*In the following viewpoint, Andreas J. Köstenberger argues that
the biblical definition of marriage necessarily involves a lifelong
covenant with God between one man and one woman. He contends that marriage must involve monogamy, permanence, fidelity, heterosexuality, fertility, and the acceptance of masculine and
feminine gender roles, where wives naturally submit to their
husbands. Köstenberger is senior research professor of New Testament and biblical theology at Southeastern Baptist Theological
Seminary in Wake Forest, North Carolina.*

Andreas J. Köstenberger, "The Bible's Teaching on Marriage and the Family," Family Research Council, 2011, p. 1–6. www.frc.org. Copyright © 2011 by Family Research Council. A longer version of this booklet was published by the Family Research Council under the title "The Bible's Teaching on Marriage and the Family." It has been adapted and
reprinted with permission.

As you read, consider the following questions:

1. According to Köstenberger, how are marriage and the family regularly viewed in today's world?

2. What six negative consequences has ideal marriage suffered as a result of sin, according to Köstenberger?

3. In what two ways does the author claim that homosexuality falls short of meeting God's design for marriage?

The Bible defines "family" in a narrow sense as *the union of one man and one woman in matrimony which is normally blessed with one or several natural or adopted children.* In a broad sense, this family also includes any other persons related by blood (the extended family). In the book of Genesis, we read that God in the beginning created first a man (Adam) to exercise dominion over his creation and subsequently a woman (Eve) as the man's "suitable helper." Then, the inspired writer remarks, "Therefore a man shall leave his father and his mother and hold fast to his wife, and they shall become one flesh." This verse sets forth the biblical pattern as it was instituted by God at the beginning: one man is united to one woman in matrimony, and the two form one new natural family. In this regard, "become one flesh" not only refers to the establishment of one new family but also to the husband and wife's sexual union leading to the procreation of offspring. This, in turn, is in keeping with God's original command to the first human couple to "be fruitful and multiply and fill the earth and subdue it and have dominion" over all of creation.

These aspects of marriage—the complementarity of male and female, and the irreplaceable role of male-female relations in reproducing the human race—are part of the original order of creation, and are evident to all human beings from the enduring order of nature. These common elements of marriage are at the heart of our civil laws defining and regulating marriage. Therefore, people of all cultures and religions—including those who lack faith in God, Christ, or the Bible—are capable of participating in the institution of marriage. However, we who are Christians believe that the fullest understanding of God's will for marriage can be derived from a careful examination of scriptural teachings. It is incumbent upon the church to educate both itself and the larger culture regarding the full breadth and depth of God's intentions for marriage.

The Covenant of Marriage

Today, marriage and the family are regularly viewed as social conventions that can be entered into and severed by the marital partners at will. As long as a given marriage relationship meets the needs of both individuals involved and is considered advantageous by both sides, the marriage is worth sustaining. If one or both partners decide that they will be better off by breaking up the marriage and entering into a new, better marital union, nothing can legitimately keep them from pursuing their self-interest, self-realization, and self-fulfillment. To be sure, there is talk about the cost of divorce and the toll exerted on the children caught up in the marital separation of their parents, but even such a toll is considered to be worth paying in order to safeguard the most cherished principles of our independent-minded, freedom-worshipping, individual rights–exalting culture. If one or both marriage partners want to get out of the marriage, nothing should hold them back, or else the culture's supreme values—individual choice and libertarian freedom—are not given their due.

Marriage Is Divine, Not Merely Human

By contrast, the Bible makes clear that, at the root, marriage and the family are not human conventions based merely on a temporary consensus and time-honored tradition. Instead, Scripture teaches that family was God's idea and that marriage is a divine, not merely human, institution. The implication of this truth is significant indeed, for this means that humans are not free to renegotiate or redefine marriage and the family in any way they choose but that they are called to preserve and respect what has been divinely instituted. This is in keeping with Jesus' words, uttered when his contemporaries asked him about the permissibility of divorce: "What therefore God has joined together let not man separate." For this reason, marriage is far more than a human social contract; it is a divinely instituted covenant.

But what is a "covenant"? In essence, a covenant is a contract between two parties that is established before God as a witness, a contract whose permanence is ultimately safeguarded by none other than God himself. In this sense, marriage is a covenant: it is entered into by the husband and the wife before God as a witness. Because it is ultimately *God* who has joined the marriage partners together, the husband and the wife vow to each other abiding loyalty and fidelity "till death do us part." Rightly understood, therefore, a marriage entered into before God involves three persons: a husband, a wife, and God. For this reason, it is not self-interest, human advantage, or an unfettered commitment to personal freedom that governs the marriage relationship, but the husband and wife's joint commitment to conduct their marriage based on God's design and sovereign plan.

The Five Principles of Marriage

Marriage is a covenant, a sacred bond between a man and a woman instituted by and publicly entered into before God and normally consummated by sexual intercourse. God's plan for the marriage covenant involves at least the following five vital principles:

1. *The permanence of marriage*: Marriage is intended to be permanent, since it was established by God. Marriage represents a serious commitment that should not be entered into lightly or unadvisedly. It involves a solemn

promise or pledge, not merely to one's marriage partner, but before God. Divorce is not permitted except in a very limited number of biblically prescribed circumstances.

2. *The sacredness of marriage*: Marriage is not merely a human agreement between two consenting individuals (a "civil union"); it is a relationship before and under God. Hence, a "same-sex marriage" is an oxymoron, a contradiction in terms. Since Scripture universally condemns homosexual relationships God will never sanction a marital bond between two members of the same sex.

3. *The intimacy of marriage*: Marriage is the most intimate of all human relationships, uniting a man and a woman in a "one-flesh" union. Marriage involves "leaving" one's family of origin and "being united" to one's spouse, which signifies the establishment of a new family unit distinct from the two originating families. While "one flesh" suggests sexual intercourse and normally procreation, at its very heart the concept entails the establishment of a new kinship relationship between two previously unrelated individuals (and families) by the most intimate of human bonds.

4. *The mutuality of marriage*: Marriage is a relationship of free self-giving of one human being to another. The marriage partners are to be first and foremost concerned about the wellbeing of the other person and to be committed to each other in steadfast love and devotion. This involves the need for forgiveness and restoration of the relationship in the case of sin. Mutuality, however, does not mean sameness in role. Scripture is clear that wives are to submit to their husbands and to serve as their "suitable helpers," while husbands are to bear the ultimate responsibility for the marriage before God.

5. *The exclusiveness of marriage*: Marriage is not only permanent, sacred, intimate, and mutual; it is also exclusive. This means that no other human relationship must interfere with the marriage commitment between husband and wife. For this reason, Jesus treated sexual immorality of a married person, including even a husband's lustful thoughts, with utmost seriousness. For the same reason, premarital sex is also illegitimate, since it violates the exclusive claims of one's future spouse. As the Song of Solomon makes clear, only in the secure context of an exclusive marital bond can free and complete giving of oneself in marriage take place.

Six Negative Consequences of Sin

Knowing the divine ideal for marriage, and aware that marriage and the family are divine institutions, we are now able to move from God's creation of man and woman and his institution of marriage to the Fall of humanity and its negative consequences on the marriage relationship. As a study of biblical history shows, humanity's rebellion against the Creator's purposes led to at least the following six negative consequences: (1) polygamy; (2) divorce; (3) adultery; (4) homosexuality; (5) sterility; and (6) gender role confusion.

The first shortcoming, *polygamy*—more specifically, polygyny, marrying multiple wives—violates God's instituted pattern of marital monogamy. While it was certainly within God's prerogative and power to make more than one wife for the man, God only made Eve. Yet within six generations after the fall of humanity, barely after Adam had died, Lamech took two wives. Later, prominent men in Israel's history such as Abraham, Esau, Jacob, Gideon, Elkanah, David, Solomon, and others engaged in polygamy. However, not only did polygamous marriage fall short of God's original design, it regularly resulted in disruptive favoritism, jealousy between competing wives, and decline into idolatry.

The second compromise of God's ideal for marriage was *divorce*, which disrupted the permanence of marriage. While divorce became so common that it had to be regulated in the Mosaic code, the Bible makes clear that God hates divorce. Divorce is also used repeatedly as an analogy for spiritual apostasy.

A third shortcoming was *adultery*, the breaking of one's marriage vows. The Decalogue stipulates explicitly, "You shall not commit adultery." An egregious case of adultery was David's sin with Bathsheba. In cases such as these, the principle of marital fidelity to one's marriage partner was compromised. The Book of Proverbs calls adultery both foolish and dangerous. In the Old Testament, adultery is frequently used as an analogy to depict the spiritual unfaithfulness of God's people Israel.

Homosexuality, fourth, marks another falling away from God's creation purposes in that it violates the divine will for marriage to be between one man and one woman. As Genesis 2:24 stipulates, "A *man* [masculine] shall leave his father and his mother and hold fast to his *wife* [feminine], and the two shall become one flesh." Heterosexuality is the only possible arrangement for marriage, as the Creator has commanded and expects married couples to "be fruitful and multiply and fill the earth." Since homosexuality involves same-sex intercourse that cannot lead to procreation, it is unnatural and cannot logically entail the possibility of marriage.

A fifth shortcoming of God's ideal for marriage is *sterility*, which falls short of the fertility desired by the Creator. Fertility is implicit in the biblical reference to the "one flesh" union. At times, lack of fertility is said in the Old Testament to be the result of personal sin, while on other occasions sterility is presented as a simple fact of (fallen) nature. However, God is often shown to answer prayers for fertility offered by his people in faith.

Gender role confusion is a sixth and final result of humanity's rebellion against the Creator. Where God's design for man and woman to be distinct yet complementary partners in procreation and stewardship of God's earth is diluted, people will inexorably be confused about what it means to be masculine or feminine, and the lines between the two sexes made by God will increasingly be blurred.

Despite the above-mentioned ways in which God's original design for marriage and the family was compromised, however, the Bible in the Old Testament continues to extol the virtues of the excellent wife and to celebrate the beauty of sex in marriage.

Restoring God's Original Design

The New Testament teaches that the restoration of God's original design for marriage in Christ is part of God's realignment of all things under Christ's authority and lordship. In the book of Ephesians, we read that it is God's purpose "to bring all things in heaven and on earth together under one head, even Christ." Thus marriage is not an end in itself but part of God's end-time restoration of all things in the person of Jesus Christ. Part of this restoration is that all evil powers are brought under control and are submitted to the supreme authority of Christ. Later on in the same letter, Paul addresses the subject of marriage in general, and marital roles in particular, within the larger context of believers needing to be filled with the Holy Spirit.

What is the biblical pattern for marriage? This is best seen in a close study of the pre-eminent passage on marital roles in the New Testament, Ephesians 5:21–33. In this passage, instructions are given to both husbands and wives in form of a "house table," which features commands given first to the person under authority followed by instructions for the person in

The Importance of Gender in Marriage

If sexual complementarity is eliminated as an essential characteristic of marriage, then no principle limits civil marriage to monogamous couples.

Supporters of redefinition use the following analogy: Laws defining marriage as a union of a man and a woman are unjust—fail to treat people equally—exactly like laws that prevented interracial marriage. Yet such appeals beg the question of what is essential to marriage. They assume exactly what is in dispute: that gender is as irrelevant as race in state recognition of marriage. However, race has nothing to with marriage, and racist laws kept the races apart. Marriage has everything to do with men and women, husbands and wives, mothers and fathers and children, and that is why principle-based policy has defined marriage as the union of one man and one woman.

Marriage must be color-blind, but it cannot be gender-blind. The color of two people's skin has nothing to do with what kind of marital bond they have. However, the sexual difference between a man and a woman is central to what marriage is. Men and women regardless of their race can unite in marriage, and children regardless of their race need moms and dads. To acknowledge such facts requires an understanding of what, at an essential level, makes a marriage.

Ryan T. Anderson, Backgrounder *(blog), no. 2775, March 11, 2013. The Heritage Foundation. www.heritage.org.*

a position of authority. In keeping with this pattern, the passage addresses first wives, then husbands; first children, then parents; and first slaves, and then masters.

Wives, for their part, are called to submit to their own husbands, as to the Lord. As the church submits to Christ, so wives should to their husbands in everything. Husbands, in turn, are to love their wives as Christ loved the church and gave himself up for her. They are to provide for their wives both physically and spiritually and to cherish them as God's special provision for them. As Christian husbands and wives live out these marital roles, God's original creation design for marriage will be fulfilled once again: "Therefore a man shall leave his father and mother and hold fast to his wife, and the two shall become one flesh."

As mentioned, this pattern of headship and submission is placed within the larger context of Christ's headship over all other powers, which Paul addresses at the beginning of his letter to the Ephesians. Paul returns to this subject at the end of his epistle, where he urges all Christians—including husbands and wives, parents and children—to put on the "whole armor of God" so they can stand against the devil. In this warfare, believers' struggle is not against flesh and blood, but against the evil supernatural. Armed with truth, righteousness, the gospel, faith, salvation, and God's word, they will be able to stand firm and resist the devil "in the evil day." The reality of the power of Satan and his forces explains at least in part why there is so much conflict in many marriages and families today. It also helps account for the widespread nature of divorce and the massive assault on marriage as an institution in our contemporary culture. . . .

The Issue of Homosexuality

What does the Bible teach on the subject of homosexuality? As mentioned, the Genesis creation account stipulates heterosexual, not homosexual, marriage as God's original design. Homosexuality falls short in several critical ways. First, homosexual relationships fall short in the area of *procreation*, since they are by their very nature not able to fulfill God's creation mandate for humanity to be fruitful, multiply, and fill the earth.

Second, homosexuality also violates another cardinal underlying principle of God's creation design for human relationships, namely that of *complementarity*. The very fact that in some homosexual relationships one partner takes on a male and the other a female role (attested by two different Greek words for homosexuality in the New Testament) provides indirect support for the complementarity inherent in the divine creation design. . . .

The contemporary culture is in a deep crisis regarding marriage and family today. While the crisis has important political, social, and economic ramifications, in the ultimate analysis only a spiritual return to the biblical foundations will address the root issue of the current crisis. Marriage and the family were God's idea, and as divine institutions they are not open to human renegotiation or revision. As we have seen, the Bible clearly teaches that God instituted marriage as a covenant between one man and one woman, a lifelong union of two partners created in God's image to govern and manage the earth for him. In keeping with his wonderful design, the Creator will normally bless a married couple with children, and it is his good plan that a family made up of a father, a mother, and several children witness to his glory and goodness in a world that has rejected the Creator's plan and has fashioned a variety of God-substitutes to fill the void that can properly be filled only by God himself.

> "Marriage equality is a threat: to inequality. It's a boon to everyone who values and benefits from equality."

Marriage Equality for Same-Sex Couples Would Benefit Everyone

Rebecca Solnit

In the following viewpoint, Rebecca Solnit argues that although proponents of same-sex marriage have argued against conservative claims that marriage equality is a threat, it is in fact a threat to inequality between men and women. Solnit contends that traditional marriage is based on hierarchy, with men having power over women. Solnit claims that allowing same-sex couples to marry will upend these entrenched gender roles, helping to create more equality for everyone. Solnit is a writer in San Francisco, California.

As you read, consider the following questions:

1. In Great Britain, according to Solnit, property in marriage belonged to the husband until what laws were passed?

2. Feminism has made same-sex marriage possible by doing what, in the author's opinion?

3. What is conservatives' real objection to same-sex marriage, in Solnit's view?

For a long time, the advocates of same-sex marriage have been saying that such unions pose no threat, contradicting the conservatives who say such unions are a threat to traditional marriage. Maybe the conservatives are right, and maybe we should celebrate that threat rather than denying it. The marriage of two men or two women doesn't impact any man-and-woman marriage directly. But metaphysically it could.

The History of Legal Marriage

To understand how, you need to look at what traditional marriage is. And at the ways in which both sides are dissembling: the advocates by denying, or more likely overlooking the threat, and the conservatives by being coy about what it's a threat to.

Recently a lot of Americans have swapped the awkward phrase "same-sex marriage" for the term "marriage equality". The phrase is ordinarily employed to mean that same-sex couples will have the rights different-sexed couples do. But it could also mean that marriage is between equals. That's not what traditional marriage was. Throughout much of its history in the west, the laws defining marriage made the husband essentially an owner and the wife a possession.

The British judge William Blackstone wrote in 1765, "By marriage, the husband and wife are one person in law: that is, the very being or legal existence of the woman is suspended during the marriage, or at least is incorporated and consolidated into that of the husband . . ." Under such rules, a woman's life was dependent on the disposition of her husband, and though there were kind as well as unkind husbands then, rights are more reliable than the kindness of someone who holds absolute power over you. And rights were a long way off.

Until Britain's Married Women's Property Acts of 1870 and 1882, everything belonged to the husband; the wife was penniless on her own account, no matter her inheritance or her earnings. Laws against wife beating were passed around that time in both England and the US but rarely enforced until the 1970s. That domestic violence is now prosecuted hasn't cured the epidemic of such violence in both countries.

A Hierarchical Relationship

The novelist Edna O'Brien's recent memoir has some blood-curdling passages about her own journey through what appears to have been a very traditional marriage. Her first husband was withering about her literary success and obliged her to sign over her cheques to him. When she refused to sign over a large film-rights cheque, he throttled her, but when she went to the police they were not much interested. That was a half a century ago, but in the US, a woman is still beaten every nine seconds by an intimate partner or former partner, and about three a day are murdered by that category of guy. The violence horrifies me, but so does the underlying assumption that the abuser has the right to control and punish his victim and the way such violence is used to that end.

The [2013] case in Cleveland, Ohio, of Ariel Castro, accused of imprisoning, torturing and sexually abusing three young women for a decade, is extreme, but it may not be the anomaly it is portrayed as. For one thing, Castro is claimed to have been spectacularly and openly violent to his now-deceased common-law wife. And what lay behind Castro's alleged actions must have been a desire for a situation in which he held absolute power and the women were absolutely powerless, a vicious version of the traditional arrangement.

This is the tradition feminism protested and protests against—not only the extremes but the quotidian [daily] situation. Feminists in the 19th century made some inroads, those of the 1970s and 1980s made a great many more, which every woman in the US and UK [United Kingdom] has benefited from. And feminism made same-sex marriage possible by doing so much to transform a hierarchical relationship into an egalitarian one. Because a marriage between two people of the same gender is inherently egalitarian—one partner may happen to have more power in any number of ways, but for the most part it's a relationship between people who have equal standing and who are free to define their roles themselves.

Gay men and lesbians have already opened up the question of what qualities and roles are male and female in ways that can be liberating for straight people. When they marry, the meaning of marriage is likewise opened up. No hierarchical tradition underlies their union. Some people have greeted this with joy. A Presbyterian pastor who had performed a number of such marriages told me, "I remember coming to this realisation when I was meeting with same-sex couples before performing their ceremonies when it was legal in California. The old patriarchal default settings did not apply in their relationships, and it was a glorious thing to witness."

Equality Frightens Conservatives

American conservatives are frightened by this egalitarianism, or maybe just appalled by it. It's not traditional. But they don't want to talk about that tradition or their enthusiasm for it, though if you follow their assault on reproductive rights, women's rights and, all last winter [2013], renewing the Violence Against Women Act, it's not hard to see where they stand. However, they dissembled on their real interest in stopping same-sex marriage.

Those of us following the court proceedings around, for example, California's marriage-equality battle have heard a lot

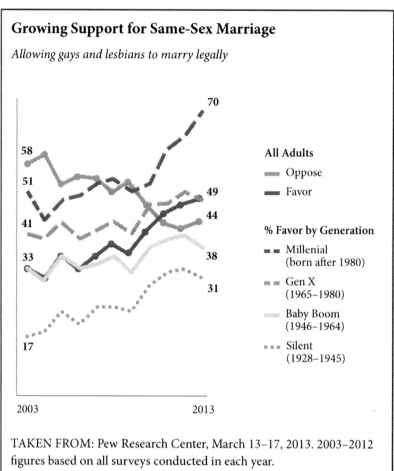

Growing Support for Same-Sex Marriage

Allowing gays and lesbians to marry legally

All Adults
— Oppose
— Favor

% Favor by Generation
■ ■ Millenial
(born after 1980)

▨ ▨ Gen X
(1965–1980)

░ Baby Boom
(1946–1964)

▪ ▪ ▪ Silent
(1928–1945)

70

58

51

49

41

44

33

38

31

17

2003   2013

TAKEN FROM: Pew Research Center, March 13–17, 2013. 2003–2012 figures based on all surveys conducted in each year.

about how marriage is for the begetting and raising of children, and certainly reproduction requires the union of a sperm and an egg—but those unite in many ways nowadays, including in laboratories and surrogate mothers. And everyone is aware that many children are now raised by grandparents, stepparents, adoptive parents and other people who did not beget but love them.

Many heterosexual marriages are childless; many with children break up: they are no guarantee that children will be raised in a house with two parents of two genders. The courts have scoffed at the reproduction and child-raising argument against marriage equality. And the conservatives have not mounted what seems to be their real objection: that they wish to preserve traditional marriage and more than that preserve traditional gender roles.

A Path to Equality

I know lovely and amazing heterosexual couples who married in the 1940s and 1950s and every decade since. Their marriages are egalitarian, full of mutuality and generosity (and of course I've known nice men married to unbearable human beings too: being a jerk knows no gender, though power relations do, and the law reinforced that until very recently). But even people who weren't particularly nasty were deeply unequal in the past. I also know a decent man who just passed away, aged 91: in his prime he took a job on the other side of the country without informing his wife that she was moving or inviting her to participate in the decision. Her life was not hers to determine. It was his.

It's time to slam the door shut on that era. And to open another door, through which we can welcome equality: between genders, among marital partners, for everyone in every circumstance. Marriage equality is a threat: to inequality. It's a boon to everyone who values and benefits from equality. It's for all of us.

"[Allowing women in combat] doesn't make the military stronger, and risks making it weaker by undermining the factors crucial for combat effectiveness."

There Are Many Reasons to Oppose Gender Neutrality in the Military

Mackubin Thomas Owens

In the following viewpoint, Mackubin Thomas Owens argues that there are three factors that make placement of women in combat or in combat-support positions a bad idea. Owens contends that there are legitimate physical differences between men and women that preclude equal performance; that the presence of women in the military undermines unit cohesion because of the possibility of amorous relationships; and that allowing women to serve in combat positions leads to the creation of dangerous double standards. Owens is associate dean of academics for electives and directed research and a professor of strategy and force planning at the US Naval War College.

As you read, consider the following questions:

1. What percentage of servicewomen become pregnant each year, as reported by Owens?

2. What is the glue of unit cohesion, according to the author?

3. Owens claims that two decades ago the US Military Academy identified how many physical differences between men and women?

For over two decades, I have been arguing against the idea of placing American women in combat or in support positions associated with direct ground combat. I base my position on three factors. First, there are substantial physical differences between men and women that place the latter at a distinct disadvantage when it comes to ground combat. Second, men treat women differently than they treat other men. This can undermine the comradeship upon which the unit cohesion necessary to success on the battlefield depends. Finally, the presence of women leads to double standards that seriously erode morale and performance. In other words, men and women are not interchangeable.

Physical Differences

The average female soldier, sailor, airman, and Marine is about five inches shorter than her male counterpart and has half the upper body strength, lower aerobic capacity (at her physical peak between the ages of 20 and 30, the average woman has the aerobic capacity of a 50-year-old male), and 37 percent less muscle mass. She has a lighter skeleton, which means that the physical strain on her body from carrying the heavy loads that are the lot of the infantryman may cause permanent damage.

But can't these differences be reduced? In the past, gender politics has made it difficult—if not impossible—to ascertain exactly what can be done to improve the performance of women, because advocates of gender equity understand that the establishment of objective strength criteria would have a deleterious effect on their demand to open the infantry to women. Several years ago, the Army attempted to establish such strength standards and pretests for each military occupational specialty, but those efforts were abandoned when studies showed that not enough women would meet the standards proposed for many Army jobs. Funding subsequently was denied for a study about remedial strength training for women.

Anatomical differences between men and women are as important as strength differences. A woman cannot urinate standing up. Most important, she tends, particularly if she is under the age of 30 (as are 60 percent of female military personnel) to become pregnant.

Indeed, each year, somewhere between 10 and 17 percent of servicewomen become pregnant. In certain locales, the figure is even higher. Former senator James Webb noted that when he was secretary of the Navy in 1988, 51 percent of single Air Force and 48 percent of single Navy women stationed in Iceland were pregnant. During pregnancy (if she remains in the service at all), a woman must be exempted from progressively more routine duties, such as marching, field training, and swim tests. After the baby is born, there are more problems, as exemplified by the many thousand uniformed-service mothers, none of whom fairly could be called a frontline soldier.

The Attrition Rate of Women

Women also suffer a higher rate of attrition than men from physical ailments, and because of the turnover, are a more costly investment. Women are four times more likely to report ill, and the percentage of women being medically nonavailable at any time is twice that of men. If a woman can't do her job, someone else must do it for her.

If one doesn't believe me, perhaps one should look at an article by a Marine officer, Captain Katie Petronio, in the *Marine Corps Gazette*, the Corps' professional journal ("Get Over

It! We Are Not All Created Equal"). She noted the physical deterioration she suffered during her deployment to Afghanistan as a combat engineer officer:

> It was evident that stress and muscular deterioration was affecting everyone regardless of gender; however, the rate of my deterioration was noticeably faster than that of male Marines and further compounded by gender-specific medical conditions. At the end of the 7-month deployment . . . I had lost 17 pounds and was diagnosed with polycystic ovarian syndrome (which personally resulted in infertility, but is not a genetic trend in my family), which was brought on by the chemical and physical changes endured during deployment. Regardless of my deteriorating physical stature, I was extremely successful during both of my combat tours, serving beside my infantry brethren and gaining the respect of every unit I supported. Regardless, I can say with 100 percent assurance that despite my accomplishments, there is no way I could endure the physical demands of the infantrymen whom I worked beside as their combat load and constant deployment cycle would leave me facing medical separation long before the option of retirement. I understand that everyone is affected differently; however, I am confident that should the Marine Corps attempt to fully integrate women into the infantry, we as an institution are going to experience a colossal increase in crippling and career-ending medical conditions for females.

The Importance of Unit Cohesion

The key to success on the battlefield is unit cohesion, which all research has shown to be critically important. Advocates of opening combat specialties to women have tried to change the definition of cohesion over the years, but the best remains that of the 1992 report of the Presidential Commission on the Assignment of Women in the Armed Forces: "the relationship that develops in a unit or group where (1) members share common values and experiences; (2) individuals in the group conform to group norms and behavior in order to ensure group survival and goals; (3) members lose their identity in favor of a group identity; (4) members focus on group activities and goals; (5) unit members become totally dependent on each other for the completion of their mission or survival; and (6) group members . . . meet all the standards of performance and behavior in order not to threaten group survival."

The glue of unit cohesion is what the Greeks called *philia*—friendship, comradeship, or brotherly love. In *The Warriors: Reflections on Men in Battle*, J. Glenn Gray described the importance of *philia*: "Numberless soldiers have died, more or less willingly, not for country or honor or religious faith or for any other abstract good, but because they realized that by fleeing their post and rescuing themselves, they would expose their companions to greater danger. Such loyalty to the group is the essence of fighting morale. . . . Comrades are loyal to each other spontaneously and without any need for reasons."

The Greeks identified another form of love: *eros*. Unlike *philia*, *eros* is individual and exclusive. *Eros* manifests itself as sexual competition, protectiveness, and favoritism. The presence of women in the close confines of a combat unit unleashes *eros* at the expense of *philia*. As the late Charles Moskos, the great military sociologist, once commented, "when you put men and women together in a confined environment and shake vigorously, don't be surprised if sex occurs. When the military says there can be no sex between a superior and a subordinate, that just flies in the face of reality. You can't make a principle based on a falsehood." Mixing the sexes and thereby introducing *eros* into an environment based on *philia* creates a dangerous form of friction in the military.

The destructive effect on unit cohesion of amorous relationships can be denied only by ideologues. Does a superior order his or her beloved into danger? If he or she demonstrates favoritism, what are the consequences for unit morale and discipline? What happens when jealousy rears its head? These are questions of life and death.

Feminists contend that these manifestations of *eros* are the result only of a lack of education and insensitivity to women, and can be eradicated through indoctrination. But all the social engineering in the world cannot change the fact that men treat women differently than they treat other men.

The Creation of Double Standards

The physical differences between men and women have, unfortunately, all too often caused the military to, in effect, discard the very essence of *philia*: fairness and the absence of favoritism. This is the crux of the problem. As Webb has observed, "In [the military] environment, fairness is not only crucial, it is the coin of the realm." The military ethos is dependent on the understanding that the criteria for allocating danger and recognition, both positive and negative, are essentially objective.

Favoritism and double standards are deadly to *philia* and the associated phenomena—cohesion, morale, discipline—that are critical to the success of a military organization. Not surprisingly, double standards generate resentment on the part of military men, which in turn leads to cynicism about military women in general, including those who have not benefited from a double standard and who perform their duties with distinction.

The military has created two types of double standards. The first is the tendency to allow women, but not men, to take advantage of sexual differences. For instance, morale, trust, and cohesion have suffered from the perception among military men that women can use pregnancy to avoid duty or deployments. A very contentious debate over favoritism arose some years ago over the claim that some women had been permitted to advance in flight training with performances that would have caused a man to wash out.

The second type of double standard is based on differing physical requirements. Last week [January 24, 2013], after Secretary of Defense Leon Panetta announced that the ban on women in combat would be lifted, my good friend, retired Air Force general Charlie Dunlap, a former JAG [judge advocate general, or military lawyer] and the director of Duke Law School's Center on Law, Ethics and National Security, weighed in: "Secretary Panetta's decision to lift the ban on women serving in certain combat roles makes sense so long as there is no lowering of the physical or other standards required for the new positions."

The Consequences of Reduced Standards

The trouble is that the desire for equal *opportunity* is, in practice, usually translated into a demand for equal *results*. Consequently, there has been a watering down of standards to accommodate the generally lower physical capabilities of women. This has had two consequences.

First, standards have been reduced so much that, in many cases, service members no longer are being prepared for the strenuous challenges they will face in the fleet or field. Second—and even more destructive of morale and trust—is the fact that when the requirement can't be changed and the test cannot be eliminated, scores are "gender normed" to conceal the differences between men and women. All the services have lower physical standards for women than for men. Two decades ago, the U.S. Military Academy [USMA] identified 120 physical differences between men and women, not to mention psychological ones, that resulted in a less rigorous overall program of physical training at West Point in order to accommodate female cadets.

For instance, the "USMA Report on the Integration and Performance of Women at West Point," prepared for the Defense Advisory Committee on Women in the Services in February 1992, revealed that scores for physically demanding events were gender normed at the academy: A woman could receive an A for the same performance that would earn a man a D. Navy women can achieve the minimum score on the physical readiness test by performing 11 percent fewer sit-ups and 53 percent fewer push-ups and by running 1.5 miles 27 percent more slowly than men. There is immense political pressure to prevent women from failing to meet even these reduced standards.

The Role of Women in the Military

To argue against women in combat is not to deny the significant contributions women have made to the nation's defense. For the last century, women have served honorably, competently, and bravely during this country's wars. It is my experience that the vast majority of women in today's armed forces are extremely professional and want nothing to do with the two extremes of feminism that Jean Bethke Elshtain described several years ago in *Real Politics: At the Center of Everyday Life* and that the military spends time and effort trying to appease: the "feminist victimization wing" and the "repressive androgynists."

I doubt that there is a huge push on the part of female soldiers and Marines to join the infantry. Captain Petronio makes the same point. The impetus comes instead from professional feminists still living in the 1970s and a small number of female officers who believe that serving in the infantry will increase the likelihood that they will become generals. But the Pentagon itself points out that military women are already promoted at rates equal to or faster than men.

In short, there is no reason for this change. It doesn't make the military stronger, and risks making it weaker by undermining the factors crucial for combat effectiveness.

"It isn't easy in 2013 to make the case that . . . no woman should be permitted to compete for a combat role in much of the armed forces."

Urine the Army Now: Ladies Can't Pee Outdoors, and Other Cringeworthy Arguments for the Ban on Women in Combat

William Saletan

In the following viewpoint, William Saletan argues that the objections to allowing women to serve in the military in a combat role are all flawed. Saletan contends that it is false that physical differences entail a categorical ban on women in combat. In addition, he claims that there is no legitimate reason to think that men will be unduly distracted by women in combat or that their presence will undermine effectiveness. He also denies that women need to be protected from the right to serve in the military. Saletan is the national correspondent at Slate, *an online magazine.*

As you read, consider the following questions:

1. What is the significance of the fact that combat-level physical abilities are rare among women, according to Saletan?

2. The author cites a survey by the Department of Veterans Affairs finding what percentage of women who served in Iraq, Afghanistan, and nearby countries to have been sexually harassed?

3. How many years has it been since anyone was drafted into the US military, according to Saletan?

Should women be allowed in combat? The Pentagon says yes, but Jerry Boykin knows better. Boykin, a former Army lieutenant general, is the executive vice president of the Family Research Council. Since last week [January 24, 2013], when the military announced its decision to rescind the combat ban, Boykin has become the point man for opponents of the decision. It isn't easy in 2013 to make the case that every man should be eligible for the draft but that no woman should be permitted to compete for a combat role in much of the armed forces. Is Boykin man enough for the job? Let's see how he's doing.

The Physical Difference Argument

1. Women are too weak. "We have seen in Iraq and Afghanistan that ground combat still requires levels of sheer physical strength, speed, and endurance that are relatively rare among women," Boykin wrote in a *USA Today* op-ed. A day later, in a commentary on CNN, he added,

> The slots that may be opened are in our infantry and Special Forces units. The purpose of such units is to directly and physically engage enemy forces. This can often involve personal, hand-to-hand combat in which women will now

have to fight men. These units can often be deployed in prolonged operations that can last for months. The physical toll is constant and wearing.

When Boykin talks about hand-to-hand combat and women fighting men, he seems to be suggesting that women can't or won't fight men effectively. But if combat-level physical abilities are "relatively rare" among women, rather than nonexistent, doesn't that undermine the idea of a categorical ban on women in combat? So Boykin turns to other arguments.

2. Combat missions are too gross for women. Boykin objects that infantry and Special Forces units are sometimes sent on months-long missions:

> During operations of this kind there is typically no access to a base of operations or facilities. Consequently, living conditions can be abysmal and base. There is routinely no privacy or ability to maintain personal hygiene for extended periods. Soldiers and Marines have to relieve themselves within sight of others.

So the problem isn't that women are inherently too weak to carry the gear or kill a man in a knife fight. The problem is that they might have to skip showers or pee in the wild.

The Mixing Men and Women Argument

3. Combat missions with women are too humiliating for men. On *Fox News Sunday*, Chris Wallace pointed out that Col. Martha McSally, the country's first female combat pilot, defeated her male competitors in the military division of the Hawaii Ironman World Triathlon Championships. "Clearly, some women can meet the standard" for combat, Wallace suggested. Boykin replied:

> Some women can, and there will be few, but some can. But that's not the issue I raised initially. What I have raised is the issue of mixing the genders in those combat units where there is no privacy, where they are out on extended opera-

tions, and there's no opportunity for people to have any privacy whatsoever. Now, as a man who has been there, and a man who has some experience in these kinds of units, I certainly don't want to be in that environment with a female, because it's degrading and humiliating enough to do your personal hygiene and other normal functions among your teammates.

Ah. So the problem isn't that women might have to pee near men. The problem is that men might have to pee near women.

4. *Women are too sexy.* In his essay for CNN, Boykin argued,

> This combat environment—now containing males and females—will place a tremendous burden on combat commanders. Not only will they have to maintain their focus on defeating the enemy in battle, they will have to do so in an environment that combines life-threatening danger with underlying sexual tensions. This is a lot to ask of the young leaders, both men and women, who will have to juggle the need to join and separate the sexes within the context of quickly developing and deadly situations. . . . Men and women can serve together in the armed forces productively, but that service needs to be prudently structured in a manner that reflects the differences between the sexes and the power of their attractions.

It isn't clear which attractions Boykin is worried about: the men's interest in the women, or the women's interest in the men. But a survey just released by the Department of Veterans Affairs finds that 49 percent of women who served in Iraq, Afghanistan, or nearby countries say they were sexually harassed there, and 23 percent of women say they were sexually assaulted. It's pretty obvious whose behavior is the problem. So the complaint about "attractions" and "sexual tensions" is basically an argument that women have to be kept away because men can't control themselves.

US Opinion on Women in Combat

Do you think that women who serve in the military and who want to serve in ground units that engage in close combat should be allowed to do that or not?

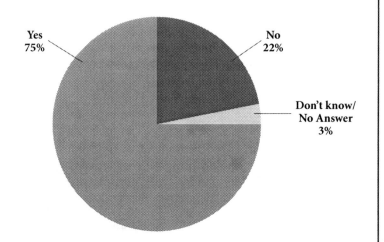

Yes
75%

No
22%

Don't know/
No Answer
3%

TAKEN FROM: Quinnipiac University Poll, January 30–February 4, 2013.

The Combat Effectiveness Argument

5. Integrating women will make it harder to segregate them. "This decision to integrate the genders in these units places additional and unnecessary burdens on leaders at all levels," Boykin warned in a Family Research Council statement. "While their focus must remain on winning the battles and protecting their troops, they will now have the distraction of having to provide some separation of the genders during fast moving and deadly situations."

Is Boykin suggesting that troops will die because somebody hung a blanket in front of a defecating soldier? If he's simply pointing out that integration makes segregation more difficult, that's obviously true. It's true not just in combat but throughout the military. It's true for female cops and firefighters, too. How far does he want to roll things back?

6. *Women will require lower standards.* "If current physical standards are maintained, few women will be able to meet them, and there will be demands that they be lowered," Boykin predicted in *USA Today*. OK, you can believe that if you want to. But here's what Defense Secretary Leon Panetta said when he rescinded the combat ban: "If members of our military can meet the qualifications for a job—and let me be clear, I'm not talking about reducing the qualifications for the job—if they can meet the qualifications for the job, then they should have the right to serve, regardless of creed or color or gender or sexual orientation."

The Protecting Women Argument

7. *Women won't be protected from combat.* In his CNN article, Boykin wrote:

> I worry about the women who are currently in the military. They have to know that the lines keeping them from infantry and Special Forces battalions will get blurrier and blurrier. What protections will they have against being thrown into front-line infantry units as organizational dividers soften and expectations change? Very little protection, I am afraid. Will they leave the military? This policy change may have the ironic effect of forcing women to reconsider their place in the armed services. If true, that would be tragic.

You can almost feel the general's tears of sorrow. Women who have voluntarily joined the armed forces—that would be 100 percent of them—might run away, tragically, if their unofficial exposure to mortal risk, unshowered men, and outdoor urination becomes official.

8. *Women might be drafted.* "I certainly don't want my daughters registering for the draft," Boykin said on *Fox News Sunday*. "And I'd like for them to have more of a choice than a man would have in a national crisis." That crisis might take

a while: It's been 40 years since anyone in this country was drafted. But the important thing is to protect your freedom of choice, by denying that freedom to women who want to serve in combat.

Why are Boykin's arguments so weak, overwrought, and confused? Because his case is collapsing, and he knows it. "Women are in combat, and women need to be given opportunities to serve in other combat roles," he conceded to Wallace. "I am no longer against that." Boykin thinks the honorable course now is to fall back and defend the combat ban for infantry and Special Forces. He's wrong. It's a bad war, General. Stop fighting it.

Periodical and Internet Sources Bibliography

The following articles have been selected to supplement the diverse views presented in this chapter.

Ryan T. Anderson — "Marriage: What It Is, Why It Matters, and the Consequences of Redefining It," Heritage Foundation *Backgrounder*, No. 2775, March 11, 2013. www.heritage.org.

Jerry Boykin — "Combat Shift Ignores Gender Realities," *USA Today*, January 25, 2013.

Daniel Greenfield — "A Gender-Neutral Army," *FrontPage Magazine*, May 22, 2013. www.frontpagemag.com.

R. Cort Kirkwood — "Women in Combat: War for and Against Women," *New American*, April 12, 2013.

Adam Serwer — "The Silly Conservative Freak-out over Women in Combat," *Mother Jones*, January 24, 2013.

Peter Sprigg — "'Gender Identity' Protections ('Bathroom Bills')," Family Research Council, July 2010. www.frc.org.

Jessica Valenti — "Why Ending the Ban on Women in Combat Is Good for All Women," *The Nation*, January 25, 2013.

Romeo Vitelli — "Is There Such a Thing as Precarious Manhood?," *Psychology Today*, June 10, 2013.

Walter Williams — "The 'Gender-Neutral Playing Field,'" *Burlington (NC) Times News*, February 7, 2013.

CHAPTER 2

How Do Gender Roles Affect Parenting and Reproduction?

Chapter Preface

A recent report from the Pew Research Center shows that the roles of mothers and fathers are converging to a certain degree. Women are spending less time on parenting, and men are spending more time as parents. But large numbers of both men and women worry that they are not spending enough time with their children, though the concern is greater among men.

According to the data collected on the hours per week spent on paid work, housework, and childcare by mothers and fathers, much has changed from 1965 to 2011 (the latest data available). In 1965, fathers averaged 42 hours of paid work, 4 hours of housework, and 2.5 hours of child care. By 2011, fathers were averaging 37 hours of paid work, 10 hours of housework, and 7 hours of child care. Mothers in 1965 only engaged in 8 hours of paid work per week but spent an average of 32 hours a week on housework and 10 hours a week on child care. By 2011, mothers were averaging 21 hours a week of paid work, 18 hours a week of housework, and 14 hours a week of childcare. These data show that the traditional gender roles—where women do the vast majority of the housework and childcare, and men do the vast majority of the paid work—are slowly lessening in extremity. Nonetheless, the traditional gender roles still are evident in the data.

On average, mothers do spend slightly more time engaged in childcare, but a large portion of both mothers and fathers worry that they are spending too little time with their children; 68 percent of mothers and 50 percent of fathers said they were spending just the right amount of time with their children. But 46 percent of fathers said they were spending too little time, and 23 percent of mothers said the same. Only 3 percent of fathers said they were spending too much time with their children, but 8 percent of mothers felt that it was too much. When it comes to how parents feel about their success in parenting, more mothers than fathers believe they are doing a "very good" or "excellent" job for the job they are doing raising children, with 73 percent of mothers and 64 percent of fathers saying this.

Among both mothers and fathers, most report being very happy or pretty happy with their lives. Only 11 percent of mothers and 17 percent of fathers report not being too happy. However, about a third of mothers and fathers report always "feeling rushed." Whether a convergence in gender roles has been good for parents is open to debate, as the authors of the viewpoints in this chapter illustrate.

| "Traditional roles for women and men [have] little scientific basis."

There Is Nothing Inherently Preferable About Traditional Gender Roles

Cathy Young

In the following viewpoint, Cathy Young argues that a recent debate about the rise in female breadwinners contained some sexism and some myths about traditional marriage. Young contends that the rise in nontraditional marriage has overall been good for both women and men, and she credits the market economy with successfully allowing women to become breadwinners for their families. Young writes a weekly column for the website RealClearPolitics and is also a contributing editor at Reason *magazine.*

As you read, consider the following questions:

1. A recent survey cited by Young found that married women who are the primary breadwinners for their families have a median total household income of what amount?

2. In what percentage of primate species are the young raised solely by the females, according to Young?

3. How have labor unions historically played a role in discrimination, in the author's opinion?

Are female breadwinners bad for America? Is caveman punditry bad for Republicans? These are the questions in the wake of a new study on women as family breadwinners and of a controversial Fox Business Network segment in which several male contributors deplored the trend as a sign of society's downfall. Unfortunately, the Fox panel hosted by Lou Dobbs fed straight into left-wing stereotypes of conservatives as chauvinistic males threatened by strong women. In fact, the discussion touched on some valid concerns: to the extent that the rise of female breadwinners is due to the increase in single-mother families, it does reflect worrisome developments. But other aspects of this trend are far more positive—and they bolster the libertarian/conservative argument that markets, not government, are the best path to female empowerment.

The Response to a Recent Survey

The Pew Research Center report, "Breadwinner Moms," reveals that mothers are now the primary breadwinners for 40 percent of American households with children under eighteen, a record high. Yet this figure is made up of two very different phenomena: single-mother families, currently 25 percent of households with children, and married mothers who are their families' primary earners, currently 15 percent of the total. In the Pew survey, mothers in the second group were disproportionately white and college-educated, with a median total household income of nearly $80,000 a year (about the same as for male-breadwinner families). Women in the first group were younger, disproportionately black or Hispanic, less educated than other mothers, and much poorer: their median annual family income was just $23,000.

To some extent, the concerns voiced on the Fox panel had to do with single mothers and marriage disintegration (with passionate commentary from Juan Williams, the veteran journalist who is black and maybe especially aware of the tragedy of father absence in the black community). Yet there was also rhetoric with clear and jarring overtones of hostility to female empowerment, even in married-couple families—with RedState.com blogger Erick Erickson invoking the animal kingdom to argue that it's natural for males to be in "the dominant role" and that anyone who approves of women as breadwinners is "anti-science."

Leftist websites quickly picked up the segment as an example of right-wing sexism, with plenty of sarcastic jabs at Erickson's alleged expertise in biology. In fact, Erickson fully deserved the backlash—which also came from his female colleagues at Fox, notably Megyn Kelly. Invoking the animal world to justify traditional roles for women and men is an easily lampooned cliché with little scientific basis (the animal world's varied and complex sex roles are hardly a model of family values, given that in some 60 percent of primate species the young are reared by single moms). Erickson also touted some dubious statistics, claiming three quarters of Pew survey respondents said that "having mom as the primary breadwinner is bad for the kids and bad for marriage." In fact, three quarters agreed that the growing number of women working outside the home had made it harder to raise children while half agreed this trend had made it harder to have a successful marriage. But only 28 percent (down from 40 percent in 1997) agreed that it is generally better for the marriage if the husband earns more than the wife. In another Pew poll a year ago [in 2012], 54 percent of men and 68 percent of women disagreed with the statement that "a pre-school child is likely to suffer if his or her mother works," and only 18 percent of men and women alike agreed that "women should return to their traditional roles in society."

Men's and Women's Views on Single Parents and Working Mothers

		Men	Women
One parent can bring up a child as well as two parents together	Agree	39%	62%
	Disagree	60%	36%
A pre-school child is likely to suffer if his or her mother works	Agree	42%	29%
	Disagree	54%	68%
Women should return to their traditional roles in society	Agree	18%	18%
	Disagree	79%	79%

TAKEN FROM: Pew Research Center 2012, Values Survey, April 4–15, 2012.

The Course of Nontraditional Marriage

Like any social shift, the evolution—or revolution—in women's roles has had its costs and challenges. We are still trying to figure out the new rules, especially for men. The course of nontraditional marriage does not always run smooth: studies find that both husbands and wives are somewhat more likely to experience psychological problems when the wife earns more. (Whether this is due to innate traits or learned cultural habit is too early to tell; the pattern is by no means universal, and undoubtedly depends to some extent on whether the spouses freely choose this arrangement or are unwillingly thrust into it.) But the changes of the last half-century have also freed women's talents and vastly expanded their choices and opportunities—and, in many cases, have also broadened men's opportunity to be involved fathers.

The market economy with its dynamic flexibility was key to those changes. Anti-discrimination legislation undoubtedly played a role in opening more doors to women; but one rarely recognized fact is that systematic sex discrimination in the workplace had also been partly the work of government. Historian Allan Carlson, a strong social conservative, has noted that the sole-breadwinner family of the 1950s was enabled by the efforts of progressive reformers and government-backed labor unions to institutionalize the idea that the male head of household should be paid enough to support a stay-at-home wife and children. The "family wage" rested on built-in, intentional discrimination against women; its decline, along with the loss of union power, partly accounts for the decline of high-paying traditionally male jobs where pay had been artificially inflated. This is a fact liberals fail to understand when they lament that the narrowing of the gender gap in pay is due partly to the drop in male earnings.

The Pew study's findings on female breadwinners attest to the power of the market and to its elastic capacity to respond to changing circumstances. That is something conservatives should celebrate—and appreciate as a rebuttal to the left's women-as-victims rhetoric.

And most conservatives do, despite attempts to tar them with the sexist brush. The day after the Lou Dobbs panels, Media Matters, the left-wing watchdog group, claimed that other Fox News hosts on the widely watched discussion show *The Five* had backed Erickson and agreed that the rise in female breadwinners was linked to society's downfall. But that was pure spin: the negative commentary on *The Five* had to do with single motherhood. At the end, after acknowledging the problem of family breakdown, co-host Andrea Tantaros noted that "every family that's not a single-mother family has to do what's best for them." What better message—for women, men, and families alike?

"Some women don't want to be mothers."

It Is Wrongly Assumed That All Women Desire Motherhood

Jessica Valenti

In the following viewpoint, Jessica Valenti argues that it is widely assumed in American culture that all women want to be mothers, with health care aimed at future pregnancy whether or not a woman intends to get pregnant, for instance. Valenti claims that, in fact, most women spend more years avoiding pregnancy rather than seeking motherhood, and she contends that a growing number of women are opting to avoid parenthood completely. Valenti is the author of Why Have Kids? A New Mom Explores the Truth About Parenting and Happiness.

As you read, consider the following questions:

1. What government agency in 2006 began recommending that women of childbearing age care for their preconception health, according to Valenti?

2. Approximately what fraction of women today do not have children, as stated by the author?

3. According to Valenti, what fraction of births in the United States are unplanned?

These days, "mom" is king. It was perhaps the most frequently used word at the Republican [GOP] National Convention this past week [August 27, 2012], where Ann Romney [wife of presidential nominee Mitt Romney], mother of five, said, "It's the moms of this nation ... who really hold this country together." [Vice presidential candidate] Paul Ryan said his mother is his role model, and [New Jersey governor] Chris Christie all but called himself a mama's boy.

An American Assumption

Republicans' efforts to woo women have become fever-pitch pandering as the party tries to undo damage from comments such as Rep. Todd Akin's remark that a "legitimate" rape victim can't get pregnant and Pennsylvania Gov. Tom Corbett's advice to women who object to invasive ultrasounds before an abortion: "You just have to close your eyes."

But given the GOP's extreme antiabortion platform, which does not include exceptions for rape or incest, focusing on motherhood as a gateway to women's hearts and votes seems misguided. After all, no matter how many platitudes are thrown around, this is the party that wants motherhood not to be a choice, but to be enforced.

In a way, Republicans are reflecting American culture, which assumes that all women want to become mothers. And the best kind of woman—the best kind of mother—is portrayed as one who puts her maternal role above everything else.

In 2006, the term "pre-pregnant" was coined in a *Washington Post* story about a report from the Centers for Disease Control and Prevention [CDC] recommending that all women of childbearing age care for their pre-conception health. The agency said all American women—from the time of their first menstrual period until menopause—should take folic acid supplements, not smoke, not "misuse" alcohol, maintain a healthy weight, refrain from drug use and avoid "high risk sexual behavior."

The CDC was asking women to behave as if they were already pregnant, even if they had no intention of conceiving in the near—or distant—future. For the first time, a U.S. government institution was explicitly saying what social norms had always hinted at: All women, regardless of whether they have or want children, are moms-in-waiting.

The "Pre-Conception" Health Movement

Telling women that what is best for a pregnancy is automatically best for them defines motherhood as a woman prioritizing the needs of a child, real or hypothetical, over her own.

Rebecca Kukla, a professor of internal medicine and philosophy at Georgetown University and the author of *Mass Hysteria: Medicine, Culture, and Mothers' Bodies*, said at a recent seminar, "Do lesbians, women who are carefully contracepting and not interested in having children, 13-year-olds, women done having kids, really want their bodies seen as prenatal, understood solely in terms of reproductive function?"

She noted that this assumption—that all women will be mothers—has led to a "pre-conception" health movement, which "treats the non-pregnant body as on its way to pregnancy."

Kukla told me that she experienced this when she once went to her doctor to get an antibiotic for a urinary tract infection, and he asked if she might be pregnant or could become pregnant. Yes, physicians have to ask to inoculate themselves against malpractice lawsuits. But Kukla's doctor wouldn't drop the issue and insisted on a weaker drug that would cause fewer complications during a pregnancy.

"Never mind that I'm a grown woman who is capable of using birth control and would have ended a pregnancy had I become pregnant," she said. "Because I . . . could become pregnant, I got this other, less effective drug."

The Avoidance of Pregnancy

This obsession with parenthood as a given doesn't match the reality of women's lives. In fact, most American women spend the majority of their lives trying not to get pregnant. According to the Guttmacher Institute, by the time a woman with two children is in her mid-40s, she will have spent only five years trying to become pregnant, being pregnant or in a postpartum period. So to avoid getting pregnant, she would have had to refrain from sex or use contraception for 25 years. That's a long part of life and a lot of effort to avoid parenthood.

Almost all American women who are sexually active use some form of birth control. The second most popular form after the pill? Sterilization. And women are increasingly choosing forms of long-term contraception. Since 2005, the number of women using an intrauterine device has increased by 161 percent.

A 2010 Pew Research Center study showed that the rate of American women who did not have children almost doubled since 1976. That's nearly one in five women today.

Laura Scott, the author of *Two Is Enough: A Couple's Guide to Living Childless by Choice*, says the No. 1 reason women give for not wanting children is that they don't want their lives to change. In a two-year study she conducted of child-free women—many prefer to call themselves "child-free" as opposed to "childless," since the latter implies an absence or void—74 percent said they "had no desire to have a child, no maternal instinct."

The other reasons they gave: loving the relationship they were in "as it is," valuing their "freedom and independence," not wanting to take on "the responsibility of raising a child," a

Maternity-Free Women in America

The birthrate in the U.S. is the lowest in recorded American history, which includes the fertility crash of the Great Depression. From 2007 to 2011, the most recent year for which there's data, the fertility rate declined 9%. A 2010 Pew Research report showed that childlessness has risen across all racial and ethnic groups, adding up to about 1 in 5 American women who end their childbearing years maternity-free, compared with 1 in 10 in the 1970s. Even before the recession hit, in 2008, the proportion of women ages 40 to 44 who had never given birth had grown by 80%, from 10% to 18%, since 1976, when a new vanguard began to question the reproductive imperative. These statistics may not have the heft of childlessness in some European countries—like Italy, where nearly one-quarter of women never give birth—but the rise is both dramatic and, in the scope of our history, quite sudden.

Lauren Sandler, Time, August 12, 2013.

desire to focus "on my own interests, needs or goals," and wanting to accomplish "things in life that would be difficult to do if I was a parent."

"Parenting is no longer the default," Scott told me. "For a lot of people, it's no longer an assumption—it's a decision."

The Stigma of Not Having Children

Yet the stigma remains. On Web forums for women without children (I have yet to see such a space for child-free men), the most talked-about topic is the need to constantly justify their decision. The criticisms are so steady and predictable that that line of questioning is referred to as "breeder bingo."

One contributor even made a bingo card with frequently heard lines, such as "The children are our future!" and "Don't you want to give your parents grandchildren?"

On one site, a woman from Virginia wrote that she mostly gets confused looks when she tells people that she doesn't want children. "I suppose it never occurred to them that having kids is a choice," she said.

It does seem odd that it's women without children who are most often questioned about their choice. After all, parenthood is the decision that brings another person into the world, whereas being child-free maintains the status quo.

And that's what Scott finds truly disturbing. She says she often speaks to women who say they didn't know they had a choice.

"I see this a lot—where women are feeling a lot of external pressure and not owning feelings of ambivalence around having children," she told me. "Many of these women end up profoundly unhappy."

Indeed, studies show that children who were unintended are raised differently than those who were planned—a disturbing situation, considering that a third of births in the United States are unplanned.

Parenthood by Force

American culture can't seem to accept the fact that some women don't want to be mothers. Parenting is simply presented as something everyone—a woman especially—is supposed to do.

This expectation is in line with the antiabortion movement and the Republican ethos around women and motherhood. No matter what women actually want, parenthood is perceived as the best, and only, choice for them.

In his speech accepting the GOP presidential nomination, Mitt Romney said of his wife: "I knew that her job as a mom was harder than mine. And I knew, without question, that her job as a mom was a lot more important than mine."

If we really value motherhood—and if it's such a tough, important job—it wouldn't be a given, but a proactive decision.

As the Republicans talk about how much they "love women"—as Ann Romney enthused Tuesday—let's remember that love isn't shown by force or coercion. It's based on respect.

| *"I absolutely hate it when strangers call me 'a good dad.'"*

I Hate Being Called a Good Dad

Matt Villano

In the following viewpoint, Matt Villano comments on his personal experience as a father, concluding that commentary on fathers often involves a double standard and constitutes a pseudocompliment. Villano claims that men are often praised for being good fathers after very little observation, raising the suspicion that the normal expectation about men is that they are not good at fathering. Villano concludes that to be treated fairly, men should be assumed to be good at parenting, just as it is assumed of women. Villano is a blogger.

As you read, consider the following questions:

1. What was the "pseudo-compliment" that Villano received?

2. In what way does the author claim the pseudo-compliment evinces a double standard?

3. What is the analogy Villano makes between the pseudo-compliment he received and the treatment of Barack Obama prior to becoming president?

It started the way all of our twice-monthly trips to Target do—the 1-year-old in a backpack on my back, the 3-year-old leading the charge, yanking my hand like a sled dog with a view of the open trail.

Some Unsolicited Commentary

We charged through the automatic doors, waving at ourselves on the video screen as always. We grabbed a shopping cart. We stopped at the complimentary sanitary wipes. Then I engaged in what my Big Girl calls "the wipedown": A comprehensive (read: wildly neurotic) disinfecting of any part of the cart she possibly might touch.

About halfway through the ritual—let's estimate nine wipes in—I noticed a middle-aged woman watching us, smiling.

"You're a good dad," she remarked, in a tone that implied she had just seen a Sasquatch.

I replied politely only for the benefit of my daughters; inside, her unsolicited commentary had me seething.

Put differently: I absolutely hate it when strangers call me a "good dad."

I mean, what characterizes a "good dad," anyway? A dude who takes the girls to buy diapers and Ziplocs while Mommy is at work? One who sanitizes a shopping cart so his kids don't pick up *E. coli* or some other bacteria? An hombre who speaks gently but firmly to his kids without engaging in behavior that could be construed as child abuse? A dude who doesn't spend his days in the local dive bar, staring into a pint of Guinness?

If this woman had seen me 10 minutes before that moment at the carts, when I gave my toddler a time-out for kicking her baby sister, would she still consider me a good guy? What if she was in our house the day I stopped a temper tantrum by spraying my child with the kitchen sink hose? (Yes, I really did. It stopped the tantrum. Case closed.)

A Double Standard

With no context—and no real basis for interpretation—the act of labeling someone a "good dad" suggests that most dads are, by our very nature as fathers, somehow less than "good." That we don't care. That we're mostly cruel.

What's more, the phrase evinces a heinous double standard: It's not like strangers compliment women as being "good moms" for doting, loving and doing normal mom stuff.

I know the poor woman at Target probably meant what she said as a compliment. When other people in other settings say the same thing (and believe me, they do), these poor souls probably mean no harm, either. Still, without exception, every time I hear the phrase it comes across as a condescending commentary on fatherhood, and a patronizing pot-shot at me—a work-at-home father who cares for his kids the way any self-respecting parent would.

Analogous to a Racist Remark

My outrage on this issue has historical precedent. Remember the days of United States Senator Barack Obama, back before our fearless leader became a two-time POTUS [President of the United States], when people described him as an "eloquent" black man? Pundits hemmed. Columnists hawed. Ultimately the consensus was that the adjective is racist, since it implies that African-Americans who don't speak as clearly, are in some way fundamentally inferior, and therefore worth less.

In my opinion, calling someone a "good dad" is no different.

So enough with the "good dad" pseudo-compliments. If you spy a father doing something nice with his children, smile quietly and go about your day. If you simply can't help your-self, peg your feedback on the kids. Note how cute they are. Comment on their good behavior. Talk about how much they clearly love their daddy.

We fathers don't need unsolicited feedback—the majority of us, like just about all parents, don't give a damn what strangers think of our parenting skills. Instead, we just want to be treated fairly. With kindness. And the assumption that most of us are "good" until we prove otherwise.

| "We need to respect men's reproductive autonomy . . . by providing them more options in the case of an accidental pregnancy."

Is Forced Fatherhood Fair?

Laurie Shrage

In the following viewpoint, Laurie Shrage argues that although few if any feminists would support policies that make motherhood compulsory, they often support policies that make fatherhood compulsory. Shrage contends that the legal definition of fatherhood that privileges biology does not protect children or families. Shrage proposes that the policies and laws surrounding fatherhood be made more symmetrical with respect to men and women, in an attempt to respect men's reproductive autonomy more fully. Shrage is a professor of philosophy and women's and gender studies at Florida International University.

As you read, consider the following questions:

1. Under what conditions does the author argue that voluntary motherhood is basically a reality?

2. Shrage contends that the courts currently use what three criteria for assigning legal paternity?

3. Shrage draws an analogy between court-ordered child support when a woman uses a sperm donor from a sperm bank and what situation?

This weekend [Father's Day, 2013,] millions of Americans will happily celebrate the role that fathers play in their families. For some families, though—specifically those in which dad's role was not freely assumed, but legally mandated—Father's Day can be an emotionally complicated occasion. And that somewhat messy reality raises a question that is worth examining today as the very definition of parents and families continues to undergo legal and social transformation.

The Issue of Reproductive Autonomy

Women's rights advocates have long struggled for motherhood to be a voluntary condition, and not one imposed by nature or culture. In places where women and girls have access to affordable and safe contraception and abortion services, and where there are programs to assist mothers in distress find foster or adoptive parents, voluntary motherhood is basically a reality. In many states, infant safe haven laws allow a birth mother to walk away from her newborn baby if she leaves it unharmed at a designated facility.

If a man accidentally conceives a child with a woman, and does not want to raise the child with her, what are his choices? Surprisingly, he has few options in the United States. He can urge her to seek an abortion, but ultimately that decision is hers to make. Should she decide to continue the pregnancy and raise the child, and should she or our government attempt to establish him as the legal father, he can be stuck with years of child support payments.

The Responsibilities of Men

If we accept the view that women do not incur responsibilities to fetuses analogous to responsibilities incurred through negligence, we must also accept this, *mutatis mutandis* [acknowledging differences], of the father. But surely, someone might object, men must be held *responsible* for their actions; fathers must be *responsible*. Child support laws, on this view, compel men to take on a responsibility which some would otherwise shun. But the claim is equivocal. Clearly, one must accept moral responsibility for those consequences of one's actions for which one is morally responsible, and one must bear the justly enforceable costs of one's actions. But just what is at issue is whether in fact men *are* morally responsible for certain consequences, and whether they may be justly compelled to bear the costs. On the other hand, the claim could mean that men, like everyone, should exercise the virtue of responsibility by acting with forethought of the consequences of their actions. However, other policies, such as contraceptive education and classes in fathering skills, could encourage the virtue of responsibility in the context of reproduction.

Elizabeth Brake, Journal of Applied Philosophy, *March 2005.*

Do men now have less reproductive autonomy than women? Should men have more control over when and how they become parents, as many women now do?

Public Policies on Fatherhood

The political philosopher Elizabeth Brake has argued that our policies should give men who accidentally impregnate a woman more options, and that feminists should oppose policies that make fatherhood compulsory. In a 2005 article in the

Journal of Applied Philosophy she wrote, "if women's partial responsibility for pregnancy does not obligate them to support a fetus, then men's partial responsibility for pregnancy does not obligate them to support a resulting child." At most, according to Brake, men should be responsible for helping with the medical expenses and other costs of a pregnancy for which they are partly responsible.

Few feminists, including Brake, would grant men the right to coerce a woman to have (or not to have) an abortion, because they recognize a woman's right to control her own body. However, if a woman decides to give birth to a child without securing the biological father's consent to raise a child with her, some scholars and policy makers question whether he should be assigned legal paternity.

Historically, it was important for women to have husbands who acknowledged paternity for their children, as children born to unmarried parents were deemed "illegitimate" and had fewer rights than children born to married parents. Today, the marital status of a child's parents affects much less that child's future. Nevertheless, having two legal parents is a significant advantage for a child, and establishing legal paternity for both married and unmarried fathers is a complicated but necessary part of our public policies.

As more children are born to unmarried parents, the social and legal preference for awarding paternity to the mother's husband becomes more outdated. When there is a dispute about fatherhood rights and obligations, the courts can use different criteria for assigning legal paternity. These include a man's marital or marriage-like relationship with the child's mother, his caregiving and support role in the child's life, and his biological relationship to the child.

The Definition of Fatherhood

The legal scholar Jane Murphy has argued that a new definition of fatherhood is emerging in our laws and court decisions which privileges a man's biological tie to a child over other criteria. In a 2005 article in the *Notre Dame Law Review*, Murphy wrote about paternity "disestablishment" cases in which men who have assumed the father role in a child's life seek genetic testing to avoid the obligations of legal fatherhood, typically when they break up with the child's mother. Her research shows that replacing the limited "mother's husband" conception of fatherhood with a narrow biologically based one still leaves many children legally fatherless.

Furthermore, Murphy explains how the new definition of 'fatherhood' is driven by the government's goal of collecting child support from men whose biological offspring are in the welfare system, as well as lawsuits from men aiming to avoid financial responsibility for their dependents. Murphy, then, reasonably proposes that judges and legislators "recognize multiple bases for legal fatherhood" and be guided by "the traditional goals of family law—protecting children and preserving family stability." Murphy argues for revising paternity establishment policies so that fewer men become legal fathers involuntarily or without understanding the legal responsibilities they are assuming.

Murphy's proposed reforms would apply to men who have different kinds of ties to a child. They would protect a naïve man who, in a moment of exuberance with a girlfriend, allows his name to be put on a birth certificate, and a man whose only tie to a child is biological. Coercing legal paternity in such cases leads to painful "disestablishment" battles that are unlikely to be in the best interest of the child or promote stable family relationships. Murphy discusses cases in which legal fathers resort to violence or threats of violence against a mother and her children when child support orders are enforced against them.

I happen to be familiar with the social consequences of forced paternity because my mother worked in the district attorney's office in Santa Clara County, Calif., in the 1970s and '80s. I remember the stories that she told about mothers on public assistance who lived in fear that a former abuser would return to harm them or their children because of the D.A.'s [district attorney's] enforcement of a child support settlement. Coerced paternity in such cases—where there has been little informed consent at the moment of assigning legal paternity—is typically costly to enforce and does not protect children or preserve family stability.

Men's Reproductive Autonomy

Feminists have long held that women should not be penalized for being sexually active by taking away their options when an accidental pregnancy occurs. Do our policies now aim to punish and shame men for their sexual promiscuity? Many of my male students (in Miami where I teach), who come from low-income immigrant communities, believe that our punitive paternity policies are aimed at controlling their sexual behavior. Moreover, the asymmetrical options that men and women now have when dealing with an unplanned pregnancy set up power imbalances in their sexual relationships that my male students find hugely unfair to them. Rather than punish men (or women) for their apparent reproductive irresponsibility by coercing legal paternity (or maternity), the government has other options, such as mandatory sex education, family planning counseling, or community service.

Court-ordered child support does make sense, say, in the case of a divorce, when a man who is already raising a child separates from the child's mother, and when the child's mother retains custody of the child. In such cases, expectations of continued financial support recognize and stabilize a parent's continued caregiving role in a child's life. However, just as court-ordered child support does not make sense when a woman goes to a sperm bank and obtains sperm from a donor who has not agreed to father the resulting child, it does not make sense when a woman is impregnated (accidentally or possibly by her choice) from sex with a partner who has not agreed to father a child with her. In consenting to sex, neither a man nor a woman gives consent to become a parent, just as in consenting to any activity, one does not consent to yield to all the accidental outcomes that might flow from that activity.

Policies that punish men for accidental pregnancies also punish those children who must manage a lifelong relationship with an absent but legal father. These "fathers" are not "dead-beat dads" failing to live up to responsibilities they once took on—they are men who never voluntarily took on the responsibilities of fatherhood with respect to a particular child. We need to respect men's reproductive autonomy, as Brake suggests, by providing them more options in the case of an accidental pregnancy. And we need to protect children and stabilize family relationships, as Murphy suggests, by broadening our definition of "father" to include men who willingly perform fatherlike roles in a child's life, and who, with informed consent, have accepted the responsibilities of fatherhood.

"Has our society reached such heights of petulant narcissism that we can actually get angry at how human reproduction works, because it interferes with our right to be mind-bogglingly irresponsible?"

Biological Realities Create Parental Responsibilities for Men and Women

Jonathon Van Maren

In the following viewpoint, Jonathon Van Maren argues that a misguided pro-choice logic is behind the idea that neither women nor men need to take responsibility for fetuses and children they create. He contends that the same logic that allows women to abort unwanted fetuses allows men to abandon unwanted children. He claims that such reasoning is only supported by a denial of the way human reproduction works and a denial of ensuing responsibilities. Van Maren is the communications director for the Canadian Centre for Bio-ethical Reform.

As you read, consider the following questions:

1. Van Maren claims that women and men have separated sex and pregnancy to such an extent that they have forgotten what?

2. What does the author think of the idea that men can accidentally father a child?

3. Van Maren suggests that society is angry with how human reproduction works because it interferes with what?

Earlier this week [early June 2013], I was asked on a radio program what I as a pro-life activist had to say about Father's Day. My answer was simple: Where are all the fathers?

In today's hookup culture, the dynamics of so-called "choice" (and, for that matter, so-called "family") are becoming increasingly messy and complex. Women and men alike—and more often, teenagers—have separated sex and pregnancy to the extent that they seem to have forgotten how it is, exactly, that humans reproduce. As the result of this, the logical extension of the twisted "pro-choice" ideology is starting to gain recognition: As political philosopher Elizabeth Brake put it in the *New York Times* earlier this week, "if women's partial responsibility for pregnancy does not obligate them to support a fetus, then men's partial responsibility for pregnancy does not obligate them to support a resulting child." For the boy-men who like to use their equipment without reading the manual, it turns out that three is often a crowd.

The *Times* article, pathetically titled, "Is Forced Fatherhood Fair?" details how fatherhood is being sprung on unsuspecting men who apparently failed Grade 8 science. The article asks what a man's choices are "if a man accidentally conceives a child with a woman." Accidentally? Did he trip and fall or something? Sorry, bro—the popular lingo might call it "recreational sex," but unfortunately you've got reproductive organs, not "recreational organs." Less rap music, more basic biology: If you've engaged in the act that reproduces humans, you don't have the right to be surprised if you end up creating a human being.

Abortion, of course, is the generally proposed solution to the inconvenient presence of a developing human being that showed up to spoil all the fun. Since Frat Boy Tom really didn't want to have a baby with Sally From The Bar, Tom can gently—or, more often, loudly—suggest that Sally go to a clinic and have their brand new, blissfully unaware offspring shredded by a suction aspirator and tossed in the trash. Problem solved—Tommy's conquest now has an actual body count, but at least he dodged having to explain to his now-deceased child how he met Mommy or mitigating his travel plans with child support payments. But—horrors—what if Sally doesn't want to allow the local fetus exterminator to force his way into her uterus and forcibly evict the baby that could well have her laugh and Tom's eyes? What is poor Tom (who hasn't even found himself yet!) to do?

The Reality of Human Reproduction

Beyond the obvious—perhaps Tommy should have "found himself" before he found himself in bed with Sally—legal scholars and academics have now come to the rescue of hapless men like him. "Feminists have long held," says the *Times*, "that women should not be penalized [*read: have a baby*] for being sexually active by taking away their options [*read: killing said baby*] when an accidental pregnancy occurs. Do our policies now aim to punish and shame men for their sexual promiscuity?" Surely, there is nothing shameful about wanting to sleep around and killing off any "accidental" children that should arise from such an encounter. "Many of my male students . . ." continues *Times* writer Laurie Shrage sagely, "who come from low-income immigrant communities, believe that our punitive paternity policies are aimed at controlling their sexual behavior."

"Punitive paternity policies," of course, being the government recognizing that little boys and little girls bear the DNA of their fathers and that this corresponds directly to paternal responsibility. The poor male students who have so much sex they can't afford all the babies are angry because they cannot be careless, and cannot sleep with women whom they do not like enough to have children with. After all, how can they be expected to conform to the novel idea that our actions and behavior have consequences, and that we should act accordingly?

Has our society reached such heights of petulant narcissism that we can actually get angry at how human reproduction works, because it interferes with our right to be mindbogglingly irresponsible? Are we so intentionally stupid that biological realities are now being perceived as legal constructs simply because that way, we can continue to chuckle that "boys will be boys" and that if those boys are lucky, "girls will have abortions"?

This is the ongoing legacy of "choice"—we champion a bright, bold future where women can abandon their offspring in abortion clinic dumpsters and, some opine solemnly, men should be able to abandon their children anywhere.

Happy Father's Day, North America.

Periodical and Internet Sources Bibliography

The following articles have been selected to supplement the diverse views presented in this chapter.

Meher Ahmad	"'Forced Fatherhood'? Yeah, Okay, Whatever," *Jezebel*, June 13, 2013. www.jezebel.com.
Jonathan Cohn	"Erick Erickson, Meet My Wife: What Fox Gets Wrong About Female Breadwinners," *New Republic*, May 30, 2013.
Lisa Miller	"The Retro Wife: Feminists Who Say They're Having It All—by Choosing to Stay Home," *New York*, March 17, 2013.
Alexandra Petri	"Science Says Males Must Dominate, According to Erick Erickson," *Washington Post*, May 30, 2013.
Reihan Salam	"The Uneven Impact of Single Parenting on Women and Men," *National Review*, March 20, 2013.
Anne-Marie Slaughter	"The Immense Value of Giving Men More Control of Household Tasks," *The Atlantic*, April 6, 2013.
Jean Strout	"A Response to Laurie Shrage's 'Is Forced Fatherhood Fair?'" *Harvard Journal of Law and Gender*, July 8, 2013.
Matt Villano	"Do Kids Care If Their Parents Adhere to Traditional Gender Roles?," *The Atlantic*, April 17, 2013.
Conor P. Williams	"Fatherhood, Manhood, and Having It All," *Daily Beast*, June 28, 2013. www.thedailybeast.com.

OPPOSING
VIEWPOINTS®
SERIES

CHAPTER 3

How Do Gender Roles Affect the Workplace?

Chapter Preface

Expectations about gender roles can lead to discrimination. Both men and women can be the victims of workplace discrimination, whereby unfair assumptions are made based on one's sex that hinder one's ability to have fair access to work, promotions, and pay. The history of workplace discrimination against women in the United States has a long history and can be traced in US Supreme Court decisions. In the 1873 case of *Bradwell v. Illinois*, the Court upheld a law excluding women from practicing law, stating, "The natural and proper timidity and delicacy which belongs to the female sex evidently unfits it for many of the occupations of civil life." Here, the gender roles of the time dictated that women were not fit for certain jobs because of their sex. These expectations were upheld under the laws as being justified on the basis of legitimate physical differences. In 1908, in *Muller v. Oregon*, the Court upheld Oregon's restrictions on the number of hours women could work, which was based on women's different physical structure that allegedly could not handle the same demands of work as men's.

Since the 1970s, the Supreme Court has held that the US Constitution protects against discrimination on the basis of sex under the equal protection and due process clauses of both the Fifth Amendment (which applies to the federal government) and the Fourteenth Amendment (which applies to the states). The equal protection clauses provide for equal protection under the law, whereas the due process clauses provide that a person not be deprived of "life, liberty, or property" without receiving the rightful treatment provided by the law. Prior to this time, the courts had generally found that the biological differences between men and women justify different treatment under the law; however, this recognition does not mean that all different treatment is discriminatory. In fact, because of certain differences between men and women, a failure to make certain accommodations may itself be seen as discriminatory.

Several federal laws have been enacted in the last several decades to prohibit discrimination in the workplace on the basis of sex, providing legal redress for men or women who are treated unfairly. Two federal laws protect against such discrimination in employment: The Equal Pay Act of 1963 requires that men and women receive equal pay for equal work, and Title VII of the Civil Rights Act of 1964 prohibits employment discrimination based on race, color, religion, sex, or national origin in regard to hiring, termination, promotion, compensation, job training, or any other condition of employment. Recognizing that pregnancy creates its own special needs, the 1978 Pregnancy Discrimination Act prohibits employment discrimination against female workers who are or intend to become pregnant.

Although these legal instruments protect men and women from unequal treatment that might be caused by unfair expectations on the basis of one's sex, it is often difficult to determine when different treatment is given someone solely because of his or her sex. For example, individual men and women in the same job can make different pay for a variety of reasons, such as differences in experience, education, and performance. Nor is an unbalanced ratio of male-to-female employees always a sign of discrimination: For a variety of reasons, all of which may be free of discrimination, certain kinds of jobs and workplaces may end up with more men than women, or more women than men. Thus, the legal protections against discrimination on the basis of sex do not mean that there will never be patterns of difference between men and women at work. The law allows for the possibility that there will be divergent patterns in the work men and women choose to do and to what extent each succeeds. What has been established in recent decades, however, is that men and women may not be treated differently in the workplace simply because of their sex. The viewpoints in the following chapter debate the effects of gender roles in the workplace.

| *"The proportions of employed men and women are rapidly approaching parity."*

Gender Roles in the Workplace Are Converging

Ellen Galinsky, Kerstin Aumann, and James T. Bond

In the following viewpoint, Ellen Galinsky, Kerstin Aumann, and James T. Bond argue that women, including those with children, now match men in desire for jobs with more responsibility. The authors attribute this convergence to increases in women's labor force participation, education, and earnings. Galinsky is president and cofounder of the Families and Work Institute, where Aumann was a senior research associate and Bond a senior adviser.

As you read, consider the following questions:

1. Among women with children who did not want more job responsibility, what percentage said they already have jobs with a lot of responsibility, according to the authors?

Ellen Galinsky, Kerstin Aumann, and James T. Bond, "Times Are Changing: Gender and Generation at Work and at Home," Families and Work Institute, August 2011, pp. 1–9. www.familiesandwork.org. Copyright © 2011 by Families and Work Institute. All rights reserved. Reproduced by permission.

2. In what two years from 1940 to 2007 were the differences in completion of four years of college smallest between men and women, as reported by Galinsky, Aumann, and Bond?

3. What percentage of married or partnered employees were dual-earner couples in 2008, according to the authors?

Families and Work Institute's [FWI's] National Study of the Changing Workforce is designed to reveal new insights about changing generational and gender dynamics in the American workforce, workplaces and families. In comparing 1992 with 2008, two emerging trends are striking:

Among Millennials (under 29 years old), women are just as likely as men to want jobs with greater responsibility.

This was not the case among employees under age 29 as recently as a decade and a half ago.

When we first started asking this question in 1992, significantly more men under 29 wanted jobs with greater responsibility (80%) than women under 29 (72%). Although the desire to advance to jobs with greater responsibility declined for all young workers between 1992 and 2008, the lowest point we have recorded was in 1997.

It is not clear what contributed to this decline between 1992 and 1997. It was a time when there was a great deal of discussion about increasing job pressure, but because we didn't ask employees *why* they didn't want to move to jobs with more responsibility back then, as we do now, we can only speculate.

Since 1997, the desire to move to jobs with more responsibility among young workers has increased. This increase has been greater for young women—from 54% to 65%—than young men—from 61% to 68%.

Now, there is no longer any difference between young women and men in wanting jobs with greater responsibility. . . .

The Impact of Motherhood

Today, there is no difference between young women with and without children in their desire to move to jobs with more responsibility.

This was not the case in 1992, when young women with children were substantially and significantly less likely to want to move to jobs with greater responsibility than [were] women without children.

In 1997, the desire for jobs with more responsibility decreased for both young women with and without children; this decline, however, was more substantial for women with children.

For the first time in the 2008 survey, we asked those who didn't want more responsibility at work why this is the case. Their responses point to concerns associated with job pressures. Among Millennial women (under 29) who did not want jobs with more responsibility:

- 31% cited concerns about the increased job pressure that goes along with greater responsibility at work;

- 18% said they already have a high-level job with a lot of responsibility; and

- 13% were concerned about not having enough flexibility to successfully manage work and personal or family life in a job with more responsibility.

Since 2002, the data for desire to advance show a clear upward trend for young women both with and without children. In fact, in 2008, the desire for jobs with more responsibility among young women with children is at its highest point since we first started asking about this in the 1992 National Study of the Changing Workforce. . . .

Taken together, these two trends suggest that Millennial women are on a similar footing with their male colleagues when it comes to career ambitions and expectations. This has implications for both men and women of all age groups at work and at home.

Over the past several decades, far-reaching demographic changes within our society have laid the groundwork for these trends as we detail in the next section of this report.

Labor Force Participation

Women's labor force participation has increased substantially and significantly in recent years.

The labor force participation of women 18 and older has increased very substantially since 1950, while participation by men has decreased. . . .

There was a 40 percentage point difference in labor force participation favoring men 18 and older in 1950, but only a nine percentage point difference in 2007. Two factors are likely to have been responsible:

- more men, and particularly young men, are not in the labor force while pursuing postsecondary education; and

- earlier retirement by men than women may also be a contributing factor in later years.

The decline in labor force participation by women 18 and older beginning in the 1990s is much less pronounced than the decline among men, but, as with young men, is influenced by their growing participation in postsecondary education, including graduate and professional degree programs.

The Impact of the Recession

The current [2011] recession has increased women's prominence in the labor force.

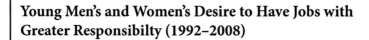

Young Men's and Women's Desire to Have Jobs with Greater Responsibilty (1992–2008)

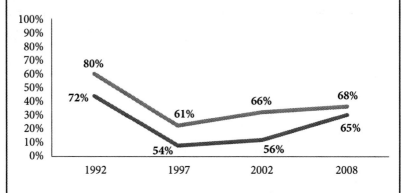

— Men under 29 (Millenials in 2008)

— Women under 29 (Millenials in 2008)

Statistically significant differences between men and women: 1992; 1997; 2002; 2008
Source: Families and Work Institute, National Study of the Changing Workforce, 1992, 1997, 2002, 2008.

TAKEN FROM: Ellen Galinsky, Kerstin Aumann and James T. Bond, "Times are Changing: Gender and Generation at Work and at Home," Families and Work Institute, revised August 2011.

The most recent data from the Bureau of Labor Statistics (BLS) indicate that unemployment rates have increased more rapidly for men than for women [in 2008–2009].

This appears to be due to the fact that men are more likely to be employed in industries (for example, manufacturing and construction) that have experienced the most severe job losses over [that time span].

Although the 2009 BLS data do not enable us to distinguish among wage and salaried employees, self-employed workers and small business owners, March 2007 data from the Current Population Survey (which we analyzed as part of the National Study of the Changing Workforce), were already reflecting the economic downturn, revealing that 49% of wage and salaried employees were women, while 47% of self-employed workers and small business owners were women.

Men are also more likely to be working reduced hours (under 35 hours a week) than in the past—from 9.5% in 2007 to 10.2% in 2008. Women's level has remained stable—23.5% in 2007 and 23.6% in 2008.

In sum, the proportions of employed men and women are rapidly approaching parity, and women may actually represent a larger proportion of the wage and salaried labor force than men by now.

Working Mothers

It is well known that the labor force participation by mothers has increased substantially and significantly in recent years, but the upward trend . . . is striking. . . .

In 1975, 47% of mothers with children under 18 participated in the U.S. labor force. By 2007, 32 years later, that proportion had risen to 71%.

- One reason why the labor force participation of women with children is higher than that of both all women and all men 18 and older may be that the average age of these women with children is older than the average ages of women and men who participate in the labor force.

- Another reason that mothers' participation is higher may be that many employed women (and men) with children have already completed their educational careers. People who are older and more educated are more likely to participate in the labor force.

Parity in Educational Attainment

Women's level of education has increased relative to men's.

In every year from 1940 through 2007, men 25 years old and older are at least somewhat more likely (in absolute terms) than women of the same ages to have completed four years of college or more. The differences between men and women are smallest in 2007 (1.5 percentage points) and, interestingly, in 1940 (1.7 percentage points) when college graduation rates were very low for everybody except the well-to-do.

A major inflection point marking men's increasing college graduation rates occurs between 1940 and 1970. This is probably related to the post–World War II GI Bill, which provided veterans with financial support to attend college. Between the late 50s and the mid-90s, men had an advantage over women in college graduation of about six to seven percentage points.

Subsequently, however, women have steadily gained ground, surpassing men's educational attainment in several areas. . . .

According to the U.S. Department of Education, women have been earning more bachelor's degrees than men since 1982 and more master's degrees than men since 1981.

- In the 2005–2006 academic year (the most recent year for which data are available), women earned 58% of all bachelor's degrees and 60% of master's degrees.

- By comparison, men earned 42% of bachelor's degrees and 40% of master's degrees in 2005–2006.

- By 2016, women are projected to earn 60% of bachelor's, 63% of master's and 54% of doctorate and professional degrees.

We do not know to what extent this trend has been due to the women's movement, general cultural change, the growing availability of government grants/loans, or other factors. But change has definitely occurred.

The Narrowing Wage Gap

The gender gap in earnings is slowly narrowing.

- In 1979, the average full-time employed woman earned 62% of what men earned on a weekly basis.

- In the early 1990s, the wage gap narrowed, largely as a function of a decline in men's wages.

- By 2007, however, the average full-time employed woman earned 80% of what men earned on a weekly basis, a big increase, but still a large gap.

It is important to note, however, that women have always been more likely than men to work part-time in order to manage their family and work responsibilities.

If we look only at hourly-wage earners (not salaried employees) in the U.S. workforce today, women's hourly pay (which controls somewhat for part-time employment) as a percentage of men's hourly pay, the discrepancy between men and women has lessened:

- In 1979, the hourly pay of women working in hourly jobs was 58% of the hourly pay of men in hourly jobs.

- In 2007, the hourly pay of women working in hourly jobs was 82% of the hourly pay of men in hourly jobs—an increase of 24 percentage points since 1979.

More interesting and quite striking: employed women 20 to 24 years old in 2007 who were paid on an hourly basis earned 90% of what their male counterparts earned, and teenage women 16 to 19 years old earned 95% of what their male counterparts earned. Although teenagers of both genders generally have rather menial jobs, teenage women may have higher expectations about wage parity than women have had in the past.

Women in Dual-Earner Couples

Women in dual-earner couples are contributing more to family income.

In 2008, 80% of married/partnered employees lived in dual-earner couples—86% of women and 75% of men. In

1977, 66% of all married/partnered employees in the work-force lived in dual-earner couples—91% of women and 53% of men.

As the earnings of women in the workforce have increased, so has their contribution to family income.

- In 2008, employed women in dual-earner couples con-tributed an average of 45% of annual family income.

- This reflects a significant increase from an average of 39% in 1997—only 11 years ago.

Clearly, many families would fall on hard times if women were not in the labor force.

Women's annual earnings in dual-earner couples have in-creased compared with the earnings of their spouses/partners over the past decade and a half.

In a 2001 Families and Work Institute report based on data from the 1997 National Study of the Changing Work-force, we compared the earnings of men and women living in couples. For the purposes of this study, we considered one partner to be earning more than the other if his or her earn-ings exceeded the partner's earnings by at least 10 percent.

- In 2008, just more than one in four (27%) of women living in dual-earner couples had annual earnings at least 10 percentage points higher than their spouses/partners, up from 15% in 1997.

- In 2008, 62% of men had annual earnings at least 10 percentage points higher than their spouses/partners, down from 72% of men in 1997.

- The proportion of couples earning comparable amounts (within plus or minus 10 percentage points relative to each other) remained steady during this pe-riod: 14% in 2008 and 13% in 1997.

The Motherhood Penalty

As women's educational achievement and work experience continue to increase, they are likely to have even greater earning potential and earnings expectations in the future. And as women's earnings increase, their contributions to family income have and will become increasingly important. This is particularly the case at this time when the unemployment rate for men is rising more rapidly than that for women.

It is well known, however, that "a motherhood penalty" remains—specifically, that the length of the time that mothers take out of the workforce or work reduced hours to care for their children diminishes their lifetime earnings.

- FWI research has shown that the greater responsibility employees—men or women—take for the routine care of their children, the lower their earnings. Women are more likely than men to be primary caregivers.

- A recent study by the Institute for Women's Policy Research showed that over a 15-year period, employed women, on average, earned only about 38% of what employed men earned. This gap is largely the result of an unequal distribution of family labor, with women being significantly more likely than men to work fewer hours or temporarily leave the workforce due to caregiving responsibilities. Fewer than half of all women (48.5%) had earnings in all 15 years of the study compared with six of seven men (84%), and one third of women had four or more years with no earnings compared with only 5% of men.

The demographic changes outlined above have profoundly changed how American men and women view their roles both in the workplace and at home.

> *"Most male Millennials in the workforce fall ... somewhere between 'eager embrace and resigned acceptance' [of women's advances in the workplace]."*

Millennial Males' "Lean In" Ambivalence

Peggy Drexler

In the following viewpoint, Peggy Drexler argues that males of the so-called Millennial Generation, those born after 1980, are adjusting to sharing power with women, who have had unequal support since childhood through programs to achieve gender parity in the workplace. Drexler contends that little is known about men's opinions on women's advancement since so much research has focused on women. Drexler is assistant professor of psychology at Weill Medical College of Cornell University and the author of Our Fathers, Ourselves: Daughters, Fathers, and the Changing American Family.

As you read, consider the following questions:

1. As reported by Drexler, Pew Research found what percentages of women and men put career success high on their list of life's goals?

2. What percentage of Fortune 500 companies have organized and funded women's-affinity groups, according to the author?

3. The Bureau of Labor Statistics has found what fraction of management, professional, and related occupation positions are held by women, as reported by Drexler?

Every study indicates Millennial males are an evolved model of masculinity: kinder, more accepting, not intimidated by dirty diapers, comfortable sharing power with a new generation of high-achieving females.

But how well do we really know them—particularly in the workplace? The new generation of women at work has been peeled, prodded, and parsed from every angle—their education, their numbers, their issues, their needs, their frustrations. But you would be hard-pressed to find one illuminating equivalent study on the male side of the gender divide.

The lexicon of women and work is crowded with terms like "queen bee," "glass ceiling," "burnout," "have it all," "mommy track," "on ramps," and—now—"lean in." Name one for young men.

There are some indications that the adjustment isn't as smooth as the assumptions of an evolved male might indicate. Pew research finds that young women are, for the first time, surpassing young men in career ambition: 67 percent of women put career success high on their list of life's goals, versus 60 percent for males. It's a statistically significant difference, and an even more significant shift from decades past—when the majority of women were just happy to be in the game.

All such surveys run into the same question: is the rebalancing—in this case, of career expectations—a matter of males trending down, or females catching up? Are the genders working their way toward equilibrium, or are we seeing the start of long-term trends?

Either way, for men born after 1980, theirs is a generation of adjustment. They have seen a rebuilding of architectures of support in everything from girl's sports to female-only scholarships to the broad encouragement for females to break down barriers. All of that, of course, reflects the maturation of a better, fairer society—where ability has blown large holes in the former battlements of privilege.

Reactions to the New Power-Sharing

In a *Shriver Report* article, "Has a Man's World become a Woman's Nation?," sociologist Michael Kimmel, a leading researcher and author on men and masculinity, sees distinct male reactions to the new power-sharing.

Some see the rise in female power as an "invasion." They are in a fighting mood, determined to recapture lost territory. Others, he argues, are largely indifferent to economic and other measures of female progress. For these "masculinists," it's about retrieving an "inner sense of their own masculinity." Many, he says, find it in men's empowerment groups or in the reaches of cyberspace.

It's likely that most male Millennials in the workforce fall into Kimmel's third category. They fall somewhere between "eager embrace and resigned acceptance." They think it's right. They think it's fair. But they are largely along for a "rather apolitical ride." Their support is rooted in the reality of change.

Adapting to what's right and inevitable means getting past what many see as a continuation of the unequal support this generation has experienced since childhood. Roughly 90 percent of *Fortune* 500 companies have organized and funded women's-affinity groups. The number of men's-affinity groups are a handful and largely informal. Companies talk openly about their commitment to hire more women and put them on special development tracks. Men in many organizations see flextime, job sharing, and extended maternity leave largely as gains for females.

The Choice for Men

There's an old adage that the Chinese character for "crisis" is a combination of the characters for "danger" and "opportunity." While some men see increased gender equality as a dangerous reversal of traditional gender arrangements, most men are going along for a rather apolitical ride, seeing neither danger nor opportunity. They're doing more housework and child care, supporting their wives' career aspirations, and sharing the decision-making about family life and career trajectories, not because of some ideological commitment to feminism, but because of a more commonplace commitment to their families and loved ones.

In a sense, they know the fix is already in. Women are in the labor force—and every other public arena—to stay. So the choice for men is how we will relate to this transformation. Will we be dragged kicking and screaming into the future? Flee to some male-only preserve, circle the masculine wagons, and regroup? Or instead, will the majority of us who are now somewhere between eager embrace and resigned acceptance see instead the opportunity for the "enthusiastic embrace" of gender equality?

Michael Kimmel, in the Shriver Report:
A Woman's Nation Changes Everything, *October 2009.*

It's a fair point that, by numbers and culture, entire organizations can be called a male-affinity group. But for male Millennials, that is a situation not of their making. It would be understandable that they look at these special support programs and see an unfair advantage to those competing for the same promotions.

Since there is so little about male Millennial opinion, I asked a number of young male managers their thoughts on the fairness of the new corporate rule book. These conversations—though well short of a representative sampling—found both support and questions.

Said one: "When you think about it, we all grew up at a time when women were getting extra support. It's just been part of our lives. But I think most men will tell you that it makes no sense that 90 percent of a school's athletic budget goes to boy's sports. Or that a woman qualified for a job gets moved aside because she's a woman.

"On the other hand," he quickly added, "let me tell you what I just experienced. A number of us applied for an open position. It went to a woman who was in the Women's Leadership Group. The supervisor for that position is the sponsor of the group. "You look at that, and you wonder. Is she the best candidate? Quite possibly. Did being a woman and a member of the leadership group give her just enough of an edge to get the job? How can you rule that out?"

Another had a different view. "It's not like they suddenly imported a whole new category of people to compete for a finite number of jobs. The talented competition has always been there. It's just that, now, a lot of that competition is female. I see some extra support. But I don't see outright bias. I don't believe things like women's groups and mentoring are discrimination—certainly not the kind that used to block the way for women."

The Bureau of Labor Statistics says that just over half of "management, professional, and related occupation" positions are now held by women. Smart employers who want to find and develop the best talent regardless of gender should make sure they are equally tuned in to the hopes and needs of the other half. Listen carefully. They tend to be quiet.

> "The massive shift in the relationship between women and work . . . has not been caused . . . by leaning in, . . . [but] by two major, obvious, and often ignored facts. The first is contraception. And the second is a decisive and lasting drop in the standard of living."

Contraception and Economic Decline Have Made the Workplace More Competitive

Noah Berlatsky

In the following viewpoint, Noah Berlatsky argues that it is false that men of the Millennial Generation, those born after 1980, are adjusting to women in the workplace because of recent changing gender roles. Berlatsky claims that changes in the workplace are due to decades of changes, the most important of which have been the advent of the birth control pill and the drop in the standard of living. Berlatsky concludes that the biggest challenge facing the modern workplace is not gender issues, but class issues. Berlatsky is a correspondent for The Atlantic.

Noah Berlatsky, "Hey, the Gender-Role Revolution Started Way Before the Millennial Generation," *The Atlantic*, May 20, 2013. Copyright © 2012 by The Atlantic Media Co., as first published in The Atlantic Magazine. All rights reserved. Distributed by Tribune Media Services.

As you read, consider the following questions:

1. Berlatsky argues that gender roles have been changing for the last how many years?

2. What two major, ignored facts does the author cite as being responsible for the massive shift in the relationship between women and work since the 1950s?

3. Berlatsky cites a statistic finding that the real wages of Americans fell by what percentage between 1973 and the late 1980s?

Millennial men and women face unprecedented changes in workplace gender roles. True or false?

Peggy Drexler writing at the *Daily Beast*, seems to think the answer is "true." She argues that "for men born after 1980, theirs is a generation of adjustment." She adds, "They have seen a rebuilding of architectures of support in everything from girl's sports to female-only scholarships to the broad encouragement for females to break down barriers." She then goes on to talk to some millennial men, who, it turns out, have some mixed feelings about women's advances in the workplace.

A Generation of Adjustment

It's certainly true that gender roles have been changing in the last 35 years. But when you say that the millennials are "a generation of adjustment", the implication is that theirs is especially a generation of adjustment—that they are adjusting in a way that few have adjusted before.

This isn't true. The fact is, the adjustments that millennials are making are part of a long trend towards integrating women into the workplace that began, not with them, but with the generations preceding them. In *Marriage, A History*, from 2005, Stephanie Coontz points out that "Every single decade of the twentieth century has seen an increase in the proportion of women in the workforce." That trend accelerated after World War II, when there were lots of low-paid clerical and sales jobs to fill—and kept accelerating through the 1960s.

As a result, the family and its relationship to work changed drastically from the 1950s to the 1970s. Post-war, the two-person family with one breadwinner became both possible and normative in a way that, Coontz shows, it had never been before, and never was again. In the 1950s, Coontz says, surveys showed that most Americans believed that people who were single by choice were "sick" or "immoral". By 1975, only 25 percent thought that. The major transformation in attitudes towards gender, marriage, the family and, by implication, work, happened before the millennials were born. If there is a "generation of adjustment", that generation is not the millennials. It's the folks who grew up between the '50s and the '70s—the baby boomers and some of their kids.

The Relationship Between Women and Work

What's wrong with the *Daily Beast* saying otherwise? What does it matter, really, if people do a little hand-waving about changing gender roles and work and the millennials? After all, gender roles are still in flux. What's the harm?

The harm, I'd argue, is that framing changing gender roles as a phenomenon tied to the millennials in particular obscures why those roles are changing. The massive shift in the relationship between women and work since the '50s has not been caused by college scholarships for women, nor by leaning in, as the *Beast* article has it. It's been caused, instead by two major, obvious, and often ignored facts. The first is contraception. And the second is a decisive and lasting drop in the standard of living.

Contraception is today so taken for granted that I think people forget how radically it has transformed not just women's lives, but society as a whole. As Coontz points out, in

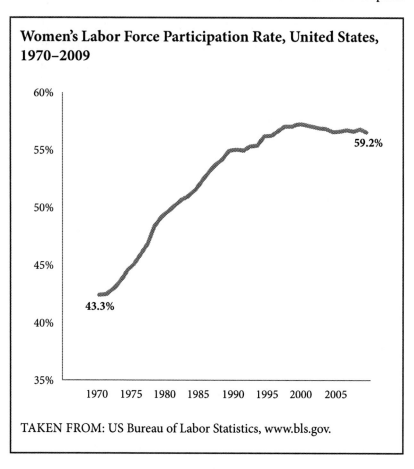

Women's Labor Force Participation Rate, United States, 1970–2009

TAKEN FROM: US Bureau of Labor Statistics, www.bls.gov.

the 1960s, "For the first time in history any woman with a modicum of educational and economic resources could, if she wanted to, separate sex from childbirth, lifting the specter of unwanted pregnancy that had structured women's lives for thousands of years." And also for the first time in history, women could control their own workforce participation. Instead of having child after child after child, women who didn't want to be celibate (which is the vast majority of women) could plan children around their career, rather than vice versa. This puts a rather different spin, for example, on the millennial who Drexler quotes as saying that women are "getting extra support." It's true that in comparison to the rest of recorded history, women are getting more support. But the absolutely most important form that support takes is not some sort of affirmative action. It's the pill—which has, finally, allowed women to compete in the workforce on an equal footing with men.

The Importance of Economic Changes

The drop in the standard of living since the 1950s isn't as revolutionary as contraception, but it's still pretty important. As Coontz argues, during the post-war period it was possible for a husband (it was virtually always a husband) to make enough money to support a wife and family in a middle-class lifestyle. Married women didn't have to work—and so the vast majority of them didn't. Instead they stayed at home and took care of the kids.

Inflation and then globalization have made the one-earner middle-class family an impossibility—and that, in turn, has meant that women, married and unmarried, have had to enter the workforce in large numbers. The impetus for women to go to work is certainly in part that people like [pioneering feminist] Betty Friedan realized that being a housewife was not very fulfilling. But the impetus was also, and importantly, that virtually no one can afford to stay at home and be a housewife anymore. Coontz points out that while purchasing power of average Americans doubled between 1947 and 1973, real wages between 1973 and the late 1980s fell by 27 percent, comparable to the decline during the Great Depression.

All of which makes Drexler's article look hopelessly confused. She's arguing that changing gender roles since the 1980s have put men and women in competition for jobs, stoking some mild male resentment. But what's really put men and women in competition for jobs isn't changing gender roles. It's economic stagnation and a precipitous decline in real wages. And what's needed, therefore, isn't more leaning in by women, or more serious listening to men's complaints about women leaning in. What's needed is some sort of effort to deal with the changing landscape, not of gender, but of class.

Not that gender is irrelevant. On the contrary, much of the unspoken rationale for America's crappy social safety net—with work-based healthcare and no day care and so on on—is the continuing image of the 1950s family as an ur-standard [that is, a primordially established standard]. You don't need day care because mom's at home; you don't need government healthcare because all the daddies work. Articles like Drexler's, which erase the past, paradoxically keep those antiquated gender roles around. The "traditional" family is always something we've *just* left behind, always something we're *just* adjusting to. The truth, though, is that these changes are of long standing, and the adjustments we need to make have little to do with the ambivalent feelings of male millennials, and a whole lot to do with policy changes that are long, long past their time.

> "The claim that American women as a
> group face systemic wage discrimina-
> tion is groundless."

The Equal Pay Day Reality Check

Christina Hoff Sommers

In the following viewpoint, Christina Hoff Sommers argues that claims that there is an unfair wage gap between men and women is false. Sommers claims that several studies show that women's choices about field of study, type of career, and time spent raising a family together explain the bulk of the difference in pay between men and women. She contends that there is no evidence of discrimination as a cause and cautions against any new legislation based on that assumption. Sommers is a resident scholar at the American Enterprise Institute and author of The War Against Boys: How Misguided Policies Are Harming Our Young Men.

As you read, consider the following questions:

1. According to Sommers, in what way are women currently protected from overtly discriminatory pay differences?

2. What is the real amount of the unexplained wage gap, in the author's opinion?

3. What is the name of the proposed legislation that Sommers opposes?

Today is Equal Pay Day. Feminist groups and political leaders have set aside this day to protest the fact that women's wages are, on average, 78 percent of men's wages. "This date symbolizes how far into 2010 women must work to earn what men earned in 2009," says the National Committee on Pay Equity. The American Association of University Women (AAUW) has enlisted supporters to wear red "to represent the way the pay gap puts women 'in the red.'" There will be rallies, speak outs, mass mailings of equity e-cards, and even bake sales featuring cookies with a "bite" taken out to represent women's losses to men. The National Organization for Women (NOW) suggests women gather together at local bars for "Un-happy Hours" where they can share their dissatisfactions. "See if a local bar, club, or restaurant (try the women-owned ones first!) will give you drink specials [where] women pay 78% of their tabs and men pay 100%."

Excuse me for interrupting, but this holiday has no basis in reality. Even feminist economists acknowledge that today's pay disparities are almost entirely the result of women's different life choices—what they study in school, where they work, and how they balance home and career. This is not to deny that some employers will try to pay Jill 78 cents and Jack $1.00 for an identical job. But our strict laws give Jill the right to take that employer to court. The claim that American women as a group face systemic wage discrimination is groundless.

There are by now many reputable studies that refute the assertion that women are being cheated out of a fair salary by unscrupulous employers. In January 2009, the Labor Department posted a study prepared by the CONSAD Research Corporation, "An Analysis of the Reasons for the Disparity in Wages Between Men and Women." It analyzed more than 50 peer-reviewed papers. Labor Department official Charles E. James Sr. summed up the results in his foreword:

> This study leads to the unambiguous conclusion that the differences in the compensation of men and women are the result of a multitude of factors and that the raw wage gap should not be used as the basis to justify corrective action. Indeed, there may be nothing to correct. The differences in raw wages may be almost entirely the result of the individual choices being made by both male and female workers.

Psychologist Susan Pinker has aptly noted that men are more likely than women to give priority to salary and promotions over personal fulfillment. Women are not as ready to sacrifice their deep interests in, say, history, psychology, or public policy—"all in order to fix, sell, or distribute widgets" or "to spend the best years of [their lives] planning air conditioning ductwork for luxury condos." Men also work longer hours and are more willing than women to take dangerous but well-paid jobs as truck drivers, loggers, coal miners, or oil riggers. (My American Enterprise Institute colleague Mark Perry has suggested we designate October 11, 2020, Equal Occupational Fatality Day. That is how far into the future women will have to work to experience the same number of work-related deaths that men experienced in 2008 alone.)

And of course women are much more involved with babies than men. According to a 2009 Pew survey, "A strong majority of all working mothers (62%) say they would prefer to work part time . . . An overwhelming majority [of working fathers] (79%) say they prefer full-time work. Only one-in-five say they would choose part-time work." To close the wage gap, women's groups are going to have to find a way to change women's preferences and life choices—or somehow rule them out of order.

In their defense, feminist groups deny that women's choices explain the wage gap. "In fact," says the National Women's Law Center, "authoritative studies show that even when all relevant career and family attributes are taken into account, there is still a significant, unexplained gap in men's and women's earnings." Not quite. Studies summarized in the CONSAD report show that when the proper controls are in place, the unexplained wage gap is somewhere between 4.8 and 7.1 cents—and no one can say how much of it is discrimination and how much is owed to subtle differences between the sexes that are hard to measure. For the time being, Equal Pay Day should be moved back from April to January.

Women's groups do sometimes acknowledge that the pay gap is largely explained by women's choices, as the AAUW does in its 2007 *Behind the Pay Gap*. But this admission is qualified; they insist that women's choices are not really free. "Women's personal choices are similarly fraught with inequities," says the AAUW. It speaks of women being "pigeonholed" into "pink-collar" jobs in health and education. According to NOW, powerful sexist stereotypes "steer" women and men "toward different education, training, and career paths" and family roles.

But are stereotyped choices evidence of discrimination? American women are among the freest, best educated, and most self-determining people in the world. It seems unsisterly for NOW or the AAUW to suggest that they are being hoodwinked into college majors, professions, or part-time work so they can spend more time with their children.

Heather Boushey, a senior economist at the Center for American Progress (CAP) and co-author of an "Equal Pay Day Primer," takes a different approach. She notes that jobs historically held by women—teaching, nursing, childcare—are paid less relative to men's jobs, even when they require the same skills. She gives the example of zookeepers (traditionally male) and childcare workers (traditionally female) and cites

Differences That Explain the Wage Gap

There are observable differences in the attributes of men and women that account for most of the wage gap. Statistical analysis that includes those variables has produced results that collectively account for between 65.1 and 76.4 percent of a raw gender wage gap of 20.4 percent, and thereby leave an adjusted gender wage gap that is between 4.8 and 7.1 percent. These variables include:

- A greater percentage of women than men tend to work part-time. Part-time work tends to pay less than full-time work.

- A greater percentage of women than men tend to leave the labor force for child birth, child care and elder care. Some of the wage gap is explained by the percentage of women who were not in the labor force during previous years, the age of women, and the number of children in the home.

- Women, especially working mothers, tend to value "family friendly" workplace policies more than men [do]. Some of the wage gap is explained by industry and occupation, particularly, the percentage of women who work in the industry and occupation.

US Department of Labor,
"An Analysis of Reasons for the Disparity in
Wages Between Men and Women," January 12, 2009.

with approval the words of another scholar who asked, "Aren't our children more valuable to society than zoo animals?" According to Boushey, such pay disparities are the "legacy of past discrimination."

Let me say for the record that I also think children are more precious than zoo animals, but I reject Boushey's point. There are vast numbers of people who know how to take care of children, but very few who are qualified to bathe and feed a giraffe. Why is it wrong for a zookeeper to earn more than a childcare worker when the zookeeper has a more specialized skill set?

There is more at stake here than having to endure another feminist victim-fest on April 20. Groups like NOW, the AAUW, CAP, and the National Women's Law Center have produced volumes of tendentious research that is taken seriously by journalists and by Congress. The Senate is now holding hearings on the misleadingly named Paycheck Fairness Act. The bill, which has already sailed through the House with bipartisan support, reads as if it were written by AAUW and NOW members during a particularly bitter "Un-happiness Hour."

Under this convoluted and impenetrably murky law, feminist lawyers will file multi-million dollar class-action lawsuits and innocent employers will settle. Liability will be based on not only intentional discrimination (we already have laws against that) but on the "lingering effects of past discrimination." What does that mean? Employers have no idea. Universities, for example, typically pay professors in the business school more than those in the school of social work. They cite market forces as the justification. But according to feminist theory, market forces are tainted by past discrimination. Women's Studies departments will eagerly provide expert witnesses to testify that sexist attitudes led society to place a higher value on male-centered fields like business than female-centered fields like social work. If the Paycheck Fairness Act passes, it will wreak havoc in the American workplace. Employers today are already nervous about making new hires. This legislation will give them added pause.

American women are not being cheated out of a fifth of their salary. They are not being corralled into inferior life choices. But dozens of women's groups have spent years drawing this misleading picture, and they have won some important converts. Last year, in his "Equal Pay Day Proclamation," President Obama said that the 22 percent difference in average wages means that "women across America continue to experience discrimination in the form of pay inequity every day." Memo to the president: Women across America do not believe that, and most will stay far away from the embarrassing grievance festivals planned for today's Equal Pay Day.

> *"Despite the evidence, myths that women's choices or other legitimate factors are the 'real' cause of the pay gap persist."*

The Gender Wage Gap Cannot Be Fully Explained by Women's Choices

Pamela Coukos

In the following viewpoint, Pamela Coukos argues that there exist several myths about the pay gap between men and women. Coukos claims that the pay gap cannot be explained away by adjusting the way the gap is measured or by blaming legitimate differences between men and women. She contends that the pay gap remains even after factoring in education, hours worked, and career path. Coukos concludes that discrimination plays a role in the wage gap and that government must continue to implement policies to close the gap. Coukos is senior program adviser in the Office of Federal Contract Compliance Programs in the US Department of Labor.

Pamela Coukos, "Myth Busting the Pay Gap," *(Work in Progress): The Official Blog of the U.S. Department of Labor*, June 7, 2012. www.social.dol.gov.

As you read, consider the following questions:

1. What is the size of the pay gap when measured as differences in annual earnings between men and women, according to Coukos?

2. Economists usually attribute what percentage of the pay gap to discrimination, as cited by the author?

3. The author charges that regardless of the impact of motherhood on the pay gap, it cannot explain the pay gap at what point?

Surely it can't be true. President [John F.] Kennedy signed the Equal Pay Act in 1963. The very next year Congress passed Title VII of the Civil Rights Act of 1964, which banned sex discrimination at work. Yet nearly fifty years later, women still make less than men.

We live today in a world where women run Fortune 500 companies, sit on the Supreme Court, and push back the frontiers of knowledge. We live during a time when more young women than men hold bachelor's degrees, and when women make up almost half of all new law school graduates. Given all our progress, there must be some explanation behind the fact that women still lag behind men when it comes to pay equity.

Myths About the Pay Gap

Earlier this week [June 5, 2012], the Paycheck Fairness Act failed to advance in the Senate, triggering a new round of conversation about the pay gap and what the numbers really mean. Research shows that even though equal pay for women is a legal right, it is not yet a reality. Despite the evidence, myths that women's choices or other legitimate factors are the "real" cause of the pay gap persist. So does confusion about how to measure the gap and what figures to use. That's why today, we are going to bust a few myths.

MYTH: Saying women only earn 77 cents on the dollar is a huge exaggeration—the "real" pay gap is much smaller than that (if it even exists).

REALITY: The size of the pay gap depends on how you measure it. The most common estimate is based on differences in annual earnings (currently about 23 cents difference per dollar). Another approach uses weekly earnings data (closer to an 18- or 19-cent difference). Analyzing the weekly figures can be more precise in certain ways, like accounting for work hours that vary over the course of the year, and less accurate in others, like certain forms of compensation that don't get paid as weekly wages. No matter which number you start with, the differences in pay for women and men really add up. According to one analysis by the Department of Labor's Chief Economist, a typical 25-year-old woman working full time would have already earned $5,000 less over the course of her working career than a typical 25-year old man. If that earnings gap is not corrected, by age 65, she will have lost hundreds of thousands of dollars over her working lifetime. We also know that women earn less than men in every state and region of the country, and that once you factor in race, the pay gap for women of color is even larger.

MYTH: There is no such thing as the gender pay gap—legitimate differences between men and women cause the gap in pay, not discrimination.

REALITY: Decades of research shows a gender gap in pay even after factors like the kind of work performed and qualifications (education and experience) are taken into account. These studies consistently conclude that discrimination is the best explanation of the remaining difference in pay. Economists generally attribute about 40% of the pay gap to discrimination—making about 60% explained by differences between workers or their jobs. However, even the "explained" differences between men and women might be more complicated. For example: If high school girls are discouraged from

Analyses of the Gender Wage Gap

A recent analysis found that specialty accounted for much of the overall gender difference in the salaries of physician researchers. Women were far less likely to work in higher-paying specialties than men were. But women still earned an unexplained $13,399 less than their male colleagues did each year, even after the authors considered and controlled for factors that had a significant effect on salary, including specialty, age, parental status, additional graduate degrees, academic rank, institution type, grant funding, publications, work hours, and time spent in research. Similarly, a recent analysis of pay differences between male and female full-time managers found that female managers were younger and had less education than male managers did. But even after researchers controlled for age, education, hours worked beyond full time, industry sector, marital status, and presence of children in the household, female managers still earned just 81 percent of what male managers did, leaving an unexplained 19 percent pay gap.

Christianne Corbett and Catherine Hill,
Graduating to a Pay Gap,
American Association of University Women, 2012.

taking the math and science classes that lead to high-paying STEM [science, technology, engineering, and mathematics] jobs, shouldn't we in some way count that as a lost equal earnings opportunity? As one commentator [Matthew Yglesias] put it recently, "I don't think that simply saying we have 9 cents of discrimination and then 14 cents of life choices is very satisfying." In other words, no matter how you slice the data, pay discrimination is a real and persistent problem that continues to shortchange American women and their families.

MYTH: But the pay gap is not my problem. Once you account for the jobs that require specialized skills or education it goes away.

REALITY: The pay gap for women with advanced degrees, corporate positions, and high paying, high skill jobs is just as real as the gap for workers overall. In a recent study of newly trained doctors, even after considering the effects of specialty, practice setting, work hours and other factors, the gender pay gap was nearly $17,000 in 2008. Catalyst [a nonprofit organization] reviewed 2011 government data showing a gender pay gap for women lawyers, and that data confirms that the gap exists for a range of professional and technical occupations. In fact, according to a study by the Institute for Women's Policy Research that used information from the Bureau of Labor Statistics, women earn less than men even within the same occupations. Despite differences in the types of jobs women and men typically perform, women earn less than men in male dominated occupations (such as managers, software developers and CEOs [chief executive officers]) and in those jobs commonly filled by women (like teachers, nurses and receptionists). In a recent review of 2010 Census data, [business researchers and publishers] Bloomberg found only one of 285 major occupations where women's median pay was higher than that of men—personal care and service workers. Because the data showed a particularly large pay gap in the financial sector, Bloomberg suggested that for women on Wall Street, shining shoes was the best way to earn more than the men.

MYTH: Women are responsible for the pay gap because they seek out flexible jobs or choose to work fewer hours. Putting family above work is why women earn less.

REALITY: Putting aside whether it's right to ask women (or men) to sacrifice financially in order to work and have a family, those kinds of choices aren't enough to explain away the gender pay gap. The gender gap in pay exists for women working full time. Taking time off for children also doesn't explain gaps at the start of a career. And although researchers have addressed various ways that work hours or schedule might or might not explain some portion of the wage gap, there may be a "motherhood penalty." This is based on nothing more than the expectation that mothers will work less. Researchers have found that merely the status of being a mother can lead to perceptions of lowered competence and commitment and lower salary offers.

MYTH: We don't need to do anything, the gender pay gap will eventually go away by itself.

REALITY: It has been nearly fifty years since Congress mandated equal pay for women, and we still have a pay gap. There is evidence that our initial progress in closing the gap has slowed. We can't sit back and wait decades more. Just this year [2012] the Department of Labor launched an app challenge, working to give women the tools they need to know their worth. My office [Federal Contract Compliance Programs] continues to increase its enforcement of requirements that federal contractors pay workers without discriminating on the basis of race or gender. And we are teaming up with other members of the National Equal Pay Task Force to ensure a coordinated federal response to equal pay enforcement. . . .

The pay gap isn't a myth, it's a reality—and it's our job to fix it.

"Employers, consciously or not, demote mothers, assuming they cannot live up to the hours and demands of the work-place."

Women Face Discrimination in the Workplace as Mothers

Ashley Nelson

In the following viewpoint, Ashley Nelson argues that mother-hood creates many challenges for women who want to stay in or return to the workplace. She contends that many women face barriers on reentering the workplace and being given the same opportunities as men. Nelson concludes that better policies are needed to protect women from discrimination after they become mothers. Nelson writes on women, politics, and culture for a number of publications, including the New York Times, *Washington* Post, The Nation, *and* New Statesman.

As you read, consider the following questions:

1. According to Nelson, what percentage of professional women will return to full-time jobs after becoming mothers?

Ashley Nelson, "Confessions of a Stay-at-Home Mom," *The Nation*, July 22–29, 2013. Reprinted with permission from the July 22, 2013, issue of The Nation. For subscription information, call 1-800-333-8536. Portions of each week's Nation magazine can be accessed at http://www.thenation.com.

2. Women with children are how much less likely to be promoted than women without children, in the author' opinion?

3. The author cites a poll that found what percentages of Republican and Democrat voters feel it is important to enact laws providing family and sick leave?

A year after I quit my job to stay home with my first child, I read Linda Hirshman's *Get to Work* (2006), which chided well-educated women for doing just that. Why, she wondered, would a congressman "listen to someone whose life so resembles that of a toddler's?" Although my daughter was napping on me, I still managed to scrawl in the margins, "Because they vote!" I was her target audience, and I felt under attack.

Since then, similar books have followed, notably Leslie Bennetts's *The Feminine Mistake* (2007) and Sheryl Sandberg's *Lean In*, published this year [2013]. While Sandberg pays more lip service to the hard work stay-at-home mothers do, her thesis is largely the same as that of her predecessors. She is quick to point out the risks of taking time off. "Women who take time out of the workforce," she warns, "pay a big career penalty. Only 74 percent of professional women will rejoin the workforce in any capacity, and only 40 percent will return to full-time jobs. Those who do rejoin will often see their earnings decrease dramatically."

The Impact of Choices

Although her argument was familiar, the unease Sandberg's book brought me was distinctly different from that caused by either Hirshman's or Bennetts's. Or perhaps I was just different. Older. The truth was, I hadn't followed Sandberg's advice. Career-wise, I leaned out when I should have leaned in. I anticipated children before I had them. When they did arrive, I scaled back my work. And recently I've been feeling some regret about that.

I was not the likeliest candidate for this position. Before I had kids, I wrote a master's thesis on the importance of women's economic independence. I wrote articles on feminism and getting women to the top. In other words, I knew this stuff. But I also knew that shortly after giving birth, I'd be moving to another city. My husband was finishing up his PhD, and there were no local positions in his field. So I left my job, figuring I could freelance while the baby napped.

Rookie mistake.

I hired a sitter, but for a time my work took a back seat to life. We moved and, two years later, moved again so my husband could take a job overseas. A second daughter arrived. Then, shortly after, I found myself in a situation I never predicted: sitting across from a divorce lawyer who didn't even bother writing down my annual freelance income. I had published well and often, but my compensation was less robust. It would barely have covered a month of her costs.

I spent the next year or two beating myself up. I had, after all, made a choice of sorts. Though divorce is common, I never anticipated it, or the vulnerability even an amicable one could inspire. So, now more than ever, I get Sandberg's point, often echoed by some on the left, who remind women that despite feminism's emphasis on choice, not all choices are equal.

The Cost of Motherhood

And yet lately I've come to believe that there is more to this story, especially given that nearly every mother I know who scaled back or quit work to care for children feels a similar anxiety about what the decision has cost her. Like myself, most never felt they were relinquishing their "work selves" completely, just momentarily turning down the tap. Many do some work, but it feels supplemental and underpaid. The climb back into full-time employment seems monumental. "I'll be 40 next year, with a PhD—I will not be an intern," my friend recently vented, with perhaps a few expletives.

The tone is melancholy, but laced with frustration and anger. After all, we hadn't spent our time home doing nothing. Children don't raise themselves, and for various reasons, usually economic and personal, we decided to devote ourselves primarily to this task, at least for a time.

And yet, while we are hardly alone—more than a third of mothers lean back from the workforce for an average of two years—much of what we hear about "stay-at-home" moms bears little resemblance to our lives. We don't care overmuch about scones. And we take care of toddlers; we don't resemble them. In fact, polls suggest most mothers want to return to full-time employment by the time their children are school-age. If we have failed, it is only in recognizing how, for mothers, discrimination and bias make this much easier said than done.

Even minor career breaks have dire economic consequences. Over a lifetime, women lose 18 percent of their earning power by leaving the workforce for only two years. A 2011 Harvard study revealed that female MBAs [those with a master's degree in business administration] who took "a job interruption equivalent to 18 months" earned 41 percent less than male MBAs.

And these are the lucky ones: the ones who find work at all. A study published by the *American Journal of Sociology* found that people were significantly less willing to hire mothers over nonmothers. Moreover, "the recommended starting salary for mothers was $11,000 less than that offered to nonmothers."

Discrimination Toward Mothers

I spoke to about a dozen women for this piece, and none of these numbers surprised them. "I feel like I'm in a holding pattern," one told me. Like many, she feels tired and underappreciated: "The other day, my husband asked me what I wanted to be when I grow up."

Until recently, she had been the family breadwinner: a lawyer who, shortly after giving birth, left her law firm for a bigger one, hoping for more flexibility. But this didn't go as planned. "On my second day back, they wanted me to stay till 11 PM," she said. "I don't want to feel when I'm leaving at 5 PM that I'm this bad person and that people are questioning my work ethic."

After repeated failed attempts to negotiate a reasonable schedule, she decided to leave. Her preference is to stay home longer with her young daughter, but her family needs the money. On interviews, she never mentions her desire for flextime, and she confesses that her recruiter is skeptical about her prospects with large, prestigious firms.

Stuck between two reasonable desires—to care for her child and to find fulfilling work—this woman is typical of many stay-at-home mothers I met. She is also a reminder that mothers who do continue working—the majority of moms out there—routinely face discrimination that, when it doesn't push them out of the workforce, makes their lives miserable.

First, there is the paycheck problem. Much attention is paid to the wage gap between men and women, but in reality it's mostly a "mommy gap." Labor statistics show that while full-time working women without children earn 7 percent less than their male counterparts, women with children earn 23 percent less. A mother is also 50 percent less likely to be promoted than a woman without children. It's no wonder there's a saying among work-life experts: "If you want equality, die childless at 30."

Other forms of discrimination are more subtle. A frequent complaint among the working moms I met is that when they return from maternity leave, they have been in effect demoted—clients moved, cases shifted. "Compared to what I was doing before, it was not important work," confessed one woman who left an investment bank for this reason.

The sense is that employers, consciously or not, demote mothers, assuming they cannot live up to the hours and demands of the workplace. Ironically, some new mothers I met privately welcomed the break, needing all the "flexibility" they could get, while also resenting the lost pay and prestige. Others, like the woman at the investment bank, felt bored and frustrated that it was so difficult to find work that was both challenging and family-friendly. When a colleague encouraged her to join a business she was starting, promising she would be able to leave at 5 and work from home, she jumped ship. Unfortunately, that promise fell flat: her flextime requests were denied, and she felt stigmatized for even asking. "My boss always suggested I looked tired because of the kids." Eventually, she left.

Family Responsibilities Discrimination

Technically, stereotyping of this sort is illegal. The nonprofit A Better Balance (ABB), dedicated to work-life issues, notes that although "there is no federal law that explicitly prohibits employers from discriminating against their employees on the basis of their family status or family caregiving responsibilities," women who are treated as less committed or capable because they are mothers are protected by laws against "family responsibilities discrimination," or FRD.

But there are three main problems with FRD. One, few women know their rights. "Moms get tons of advice about what to eat, which stroller to buy, and how to get their bodies back in shape, but what's missing is clear and comprehensive advice about how to keep and protect their paycheck after their baby arrives," observes Dina Bakst, co-founder of ABB and co-author of the newly published *Babygate: What You Really Need to Know About Pregnancy and Parenting in the American Workplace.*

But the second problem is that many mothers are happy just to have a job. Those women are tired, not often in positions of power, and scared to rock the boat. "We hear from low-wage women who can't even get an extra bathroom break or a water bottle," Bakst says. Suing is another realm altogether.

Finally, discrimination can be hard to prove. One woman I spoke with described telling the chairman of her law firm that she was getting married. His immediate response: "Pregnant yet?" The subtext was clear, the woman notes, but "I knew I couldn't build a case off just that." Her work assignments declined, and she left the firm soon after.

Proving discrimination can also be difficult when 62 percent of private sector workers are discouraged or prohibited from comparing their wages with co-workers. The Paycheck Fairness Act, recently introduced by Senator Barbara Mikulski and Representative Rosa DeLauro, could change that by prohibiting employers from punishing workers who share wage information and further requiring them to prove that any pay discrepancies are unrelated to gender [stalled in committee as of March 2014].

The Need for Better Policies

A few large legal victories wouldn't hurt either. "What we really need are some big Supreme Court rulings that shake employers the way that sexual harassment did in the '80s and '90s," says Bakst, although she is quick to point out the limits of litigation. The recently reintroduced Pregnant Workers Fairness Act, she notes, would significantly help by protecting pregnant women's right to modest workplace accommodations so they are less likely to have to resort to litigation [still in committee as of March 2014].

Another idea would be to strengthen benefits for new mothers so that if they take time off, they are not penalized so onerously. I saw this approach in England, where I had my second child. Like much of Europe, England has generous family benefits, with new mothers receiving a year of job protection and thirty-nine weeks paid leave, in some cases up to 90 percent of one's salary. New fathers get some paid leave, too, and can, during the first year, stay at home with pay for up to twenty-six weeks if the mother chooses to work.

England also offers universal preschool after a child's fourth birthday and fifteen hours of free "nursery" after their third (and sometimes second) birthday. Parents also have the right to request flexible work schedules, including the right to scale back to part time either temporarily or permanently. Employers do not have to grant the request, but they must provide an explicit reason for denying it. Finally, part-time workers, the vast majority of whom are women, must be paid on the same scale and receive the same benefits as full-time workers.

These benefits can act as lifelines for women by significantly reducing that scramble time in the United States—the time between birth and kindergarten—when many women just give up, if they don't get pushed out first. Further, when women are granted paid maternity leave, they are more likely to return to work and maintain higher wages than women without leave.

One of the biggest challenges, however, is tackling resistance to government regulation of employee benefits and access to workplace flexibility. Also in Europe, governments generally pay for benefits like family leave, but there is little political support for that here. And getting employers to foot the bill seems unlikely. While some corporations, like Google, appear to be amenable to this approach, others that set the parameters of the debate do not—and politicians seem increasingly beholden to them. The GOP-sponsored Working Families Flexibility Act of 2013, for example, is a pale shadow of the legislation sponsored under the same name by Ted Kennedy in 2007 and Carolyn Maloney in 2012. Kennedy's and Maloney's versions would have guaranteed employees the right to request flextime without penalty, as they can already do in England and other parts of Europe. Both efforts failed. The latest version, though it proposes to support employees, panders to employers instead, allowing them to give their workers comp time instead of overtime pay. It passed the House in May [but is still in committee in the Senate as of March 2014].

The Future for Working Mothers

There is some reason to hope the tide is turning. President [Barack] Obama just proposed a $75 billion plan for universal preschool. And, perhaps more significant, a recent poll released by the National Partnership for Women & Families shows that the majority of voters, both Republican (73 percent) and Democrat (96 percent), feel it's important to consider enacting laws that provide for paid family leave and paid sick days. These figures are up from similar polls conducted just a few years ago.

But until this happens, mothers must fend for themselves. When I ask Allison O'Kelly, founder of Mom Corps, a staffing organization that helps connect mothers with flexible employment, what advice she has for new mothers struggling between childcare and work, she hesitates. "Honestly, I'm a big believer in staying in, because re-entry is so tricky," she says. "But if you do take time off, do something, even if it's small— even if it's ten hours a week. Something paid is preferable to volunteer work, but if you have nothing else, then volunteer. Keep your résumé fresh."

It's difficult to argue with such a practical approach. And yet it seems equally important to reframe this issue by focusing on the hurdles women face, not the individual "choices" they make. The latter may be a salable approach, pitting women against women, but it distracts from the more pressing issue of discrimination. Moreover, while choices seem black-and-white from afar, what you learn from sitting down with mothers is that life is more complicated than that. I'm not going to argue with the woman who tried for six years to have a child and then stayed home with her for three. Nor can I blame the many who leave work because they are tired of spending their entire paycheck on childcare.

The stories I heard from such women are the stories of half the population, stories that politicians and businesses need to hear, and that women need to voice. "Show them how ready and motivated you are." This is Allison O'Kelly's advice on how to win over an employer, but it's good advice all around.

| "Federal law has not kept pace with is-
sues faced by pregnant workers."

Women Need Special Employment Protection During Pregnancy

Noreen Farrell, Jamie Dolkas, and Mia Munro

In the following viewpoint, Noreen Farrell, Jamie Dolkas, and Mia Munro argue that current federal law is inadequate to protect pregnant workers from discrimination in the workplace. The authors contend that in their current forms, the Pregnancy Discrimination Act, the Family and Medical Leave Act, and the Americans with Disabilities Act do not work to adequately protect the rights of pregnant women at work. Farrell is executive director, Dolkas a former staff attorney, and Munro a staff attorney at Equal Rights Advocates (ERA), a national civil rights organization.

As you read, consider the following questions:

1. What percentage of working women will become mothers during the course of their working lives, according to Farrell, Dolkas, and Munro?

2. The authors claim that the US Department of Labor found that in 2005, what percentage of the workforce was eligible for leave under the Family and Medical Leave Act?

3. What proposed legislation would avoid the hurdles for pregnant women posed by the Americans with Disabilities Act (ADA) and ADA Amendments Act, in the authors' opinion?

The landscape of the American workforce has undergone a dramatic change since Congress enacted Title VII of the Civil Rights Act of 1964. Women now make up nearly half of the workforce and are represented in nearly every profession and income bracket. Nearly 75% of all working women will become mothers during the course of their working lives. Women with paid employment are essential to the financial well-being of their families. Most married couples rely on a dual-parent income. In 2010, 40% of working mothers were the primary breadwinner for their families. More women are working while pregnant and later into their pregnancies. In the past forty years, there has been a 45% increase in the number of women who are working up to one month before birth.

The Shortcomings of Federal Laws

For all this progress, federal law has not kept pace with issues faced by pregnant workers. The number of federal pregnancy discrimination charges filed with federal and state agencies has skyrocketed since 1997. Over the past ten years, the vast majority of these charges included allegations of discharge based on pregnancy.

On February 15, 2012, attorneys, academics, and other experts from across the country participated in a historic meeting of the U.S. Equal Economic Opportunity Commission (EEOC) to address the troubling rise in cases of discrimination on the basis of pregnancy and caregiving. Equal Rights Advocates [ERA] submitted written testimony for the hearing. Most of the participants were uniform in their call for data collection, greater EEOC guidance on the types of conduct that are unlawful under current federal law, and better enforcement by the federal agency to curb unlawful discrimination.

While the Pregnancy Discrimination Act, the Family [and] Medical Leave Act, and the Americans with Disabilities Act have provided great support to women and other workers, many participants in the EEOC meeting acknowledged the shortcomings of these federal laws (as drafted and/or applied by courts) to ensure that pregnant employees receive modest accommodations to allow them to continue to work during their pregnancies.

The Pregnancy Discrimination Act

The Pregnancy Discrimination Act ("PDA") prohibits employers and other covered entities from discriminating against applicants and employees on the basis of "pregnancy, childbirth, or related medical conditions" with respect to all aspects of employment. The PDA prohibits employers from singling out pregnant employees and subjecting them to any form of adverse treatment when the pregnant employee is capable of working on the same terms as all other fully capable workers.

However, to the extent that a pregnant worker needs an adjustment in the workplace to continue working, the PDA has limitations. While the Supreme Court has made clear that states may require greater protections for pregnant workers, the PDA itself only requires employers to make accommodations for pregnant women to the extent they accommodate other employees "similar in their ability or inability to work."

In the absence of the appropriate comparator showing discriminatory treatment on the basis of pregnancy, pregnant workers have not been able to rely consistently on the PDA to challenge an employer's refusal to allow them sitting breaks or other modest workplace adjustments. As a practical matter, these cases are often difficult to prove, even when discrimination exists. An employer's willingness to accommodate the physical injury of a non-pregnant employee with light duty is often a matter of ad hoc practice, not official written policy. In a large company, these ad hoc practices may not be known to a pregnant worker or supervisory personnel. Even when plaintiffs have alleged the relatively rare PDA case based on a disparate impact theory, courts have been reluctant to grant relief.

The Failure of the PDA

The failure of the PDA to require the reasonable accommodation of all pregnant workers has contributed to a startling trend. Pregnant workers are often treated worse than other workers who are limited in their ability to perform certain aspects of a job. At least some courts have held that an employer may deny pregnant employees light duty assignments provided to employees injured on the job. In Tennessee, Amanda Reeves, a pregnant truck driver, sought light duty after her doctor advised her not to lift more than 20 pounds. She was terminated, even though her employer offered light duty to employees injured on the job. Similarly, in Landover, Maryland, a delivery truck driver was forced out on unpaid leave because she had a lifting restriction and was denied light duty, despite her employer's policy of accommodating similar impairments of other employees. In both cases, the PDA did not provide these women with relief.

Similarly, accommodations that would be readily provided to a worker covered by the Americans with Disabilities Act are commonly denied to pregnant workers. For example, a retail worker in Salina, Kansas was fired because she needed to carry a water bottle to stay hydrated and prevent bladder infections. An activity director at a nursing home in Valparaiso, Indiana was terminated because she required help with some physically strenuous aspects of her job to prevent another miscarriage. More and more pregnant workers are being pushed out of the workplace.

These cases are consistent with the experience of callers to ERA's Advice and Counseling Hotline.

The Family and Medical Leave Act

The Family and Medical Leave Act ("FMLA") also falls far short of solving the problem faced by pregnant workers. The FMLA allows employees who work for employers with fifty or more employees to take up to twelve weeks of job-protected leave to care for their own serious health condition or that of a close family member. It also requires employers to continue to provide company-sponsored health insurance coverage and other benefits that are crucial to the healthy pregnancies of their employees.

While the FMLA allows medically necessary leave for pregnancy conditions, the law is not meeting the needs of many pregnant workers. The FMLA does not extend its protection to workers employed by smaller businesses. A 2007 report from the U.S. Department of Labor found that in 2005 only 54 percent of the workforce in the United States, 76.1 million employees, were eligible for FMLA-protected leave. Of the 65.6 million ineligible workers, 47.3 million worked at establishments too small to be covered and 18.3 million lacked the job tenure or the required number of hours-in-job to be eligible. An even greater obstacle to taking FMLA leave is that many workers cannot afford unpaid leave for three months.

While the FMLA may offer brief protection to eligible pregnant workers who can afford unpaid leave, it only provides twelve weeks of leave. The FMLA does not provide job protection for employees who must take more than 12 weeks of leave because their employers forced them out early in their pregnancies. . . .

The FMLA does not cover enough pregnant workers, provide pay necessary for continued support of their families, or provide job protection for leaves over twelve weeks. More fundamentally, the FMLA is designed to provide time off for workers who are incapacitated because of a serious health condition. It does not fulfill the needs of pregnant workers who are willing and able to continue to work continuously with modest accommodations.

The Americans with Disabilities Act

The protection provided to pregnant workers seeking workplace accommodations by the Americans with Disabilities Act (ADA), as amended by the 2008 ADA Amendments Act (ADAAA), remains unsettled. The ADA prohibits employers and other covered entities from discriminating against qualified individuals with disabilities in employment. A qualified employee or applicant with a disability is an individual who has a "disability," and, with or without reasonable accommodation, can perform the essential functions of the job. An employer is required to make a reasonable accommodation to the known disability of a qualified applicant or employee if it would not impose an "undue hardship" on the operation of the employer's business.

The 2008 ADAAA now obligates employers to accommodate a broader range of temporary disabilities posing modest limitations on activities such as standing, lifting, or bending. The EEOC's new regulations implementing the ADAAA, for example, provides that: "[i]f an individual has a back impairment that results in a 20-pound lifting restriction that lasts for several months, he is substantially limited in the major life activity of lifting, and therefore covered under the first prong of the definition of disability."

While the ADAAA provides broader coverage, it presents obstacles for pregnant workers. Because the ADA/ADAAA was designed to cover a spectrum of disabilities, the framework to establish whether or not an employee has a qualifying "disability," and is thus entitled to reasonable accommodation involves complicated analysis. While the ADAAA broadens the definition of disability and reduces the amount of scrutiny involved, the hurdles for establishing coverage are not eliminated under it. These procedural hurdles would not be necessary under the Pregnant Workers Fairness Act [in committee as of March 2014] because pregnancy qualifies an employee for coverage.

Additionally, under the ADAAA and confirmed in the EEOC's newly issued guidance, pregnancy is still not a per se disability. Indeed, the Interpretative Guidance states: "Other conditions, such as pregnancy, that are not the result of a physiological disorder are also not impairments."

Extending the ADAAA to Pregnancy

Courts have yet to interpret the extension of the ADAAA to pregnant workers, but it is likely that courts will construe only a narrow and limited set of pregnant-related impairments as rising to the level of disability under the ADAAA (such as pregnancy-related hypertension, etc.). Not all pregnant workers will meet the ADAAA's definition of "disabled" given the minor nature of adjustments they seek.

Consider Carmen, a pharmacy worker from New Jersey who called ERA's Advice and Counseling line. Carmen is a single immigrant pharmacy worker who was regularly denied bathroom breaks that she needed because she was pregnant. Carmen suffered from severe stomach pains as a result. When pregnancy conditions forced Carmen to go on sick leave and then to the hospital, she was disciplined for taking sick leave.

It is uncertain that Carmen's pregnancy issues would meet the ADAAA's definition of "disability." Thus, whether the ADAAA would have required that the employer reasonably accommodate her need for more bathroom breaks is unclear. Yet, these are precisely the minor adjustments that many preg-

Periodical and Internet Sources Bibliography

The following articles have been selected to supplement the diverse views presented in this chapter.

Kerstin Aumann, Ellen Galinsky, and Kenneth Matos	"The New Male Mystique," Families and Work Institute, 2011. www.familiesandwork.org.
Romina Boccia	"Equal Pay Act at 50: The Myth of the Gender Wage Gap," *The Foundry* (blog), the Heritage Foundation, June 10, 2013. www.blog.heritage.org.
Irin Carmon	"Juggling a Job and Family Is a Men's Issue, Too," *Salon*, May 30, 2013. www.salon.com.
Diana Furchtgott-Roth	"Women and the Unequal Pay Myth," Real Clear Markets, June 18, 2013. www.realclearmarkets.com.
Fawn Johnson	"High Hurdles," *National Journal*, July 14, 2012.
Christina Hoff Sommers	"What 'Lean In' Misunderstands About Gender Differences," *The Atlantic*, March 19, 2013.
Stephanie Stamm	"The Gender Gap in Senior-Level Government Jobs," *National Journal*, July 11, 2012.
Derek Thompson	"The Biggest Myth About the Gender Wage Gap," *The Atlantic*, May 30, 2013.
Hrag Vartanian	"Academia's Gender Gap Persists," *Salon*, July 24, 2013. www.salon.com.

OPPOSING
VIEWPOINTS®
SERIES

CHAPTER 4

How Are Gender Roles Changing?

Chapter Preface

Gender roles have changed over the past several decades. Several social changes are likely responsible for the changes that have in many ways blurred the lines between the roles that have traditionally been seen as acceptable for men and women. One hundred years ago women were expected to be primarily occupied with the work of the home: raising children, cooking meals, cleaning, and helping with the family garden or farm. Men, on the other hand, worked outside the home, often for a wage and for an employer. Men were often in charge of making major decisions for the family and, in fact, women in the United States did not receive the right to vote until the passage of the Nineteenth Amendment to the US Constitution in 1920. Although some American families still reflect the gender roles of a century ago, many have upended the roles, partly due to the way the profile of the American family has changed.

More American adults are unmarried now than a century ago. According to the US Census Bureau, in 2012, 44 percent of all US residents aged eighteen and older were single, with 24 percent of those being divorced. Almost half of all households—46 percent—were maintained by unmarried men and women.

Parenting has also changed. Over a third of women in their childbearing years—aged fifteen to fifty—who gave birth in 2011 were widowed, divorced, or never married. In 2011 there were 6.7 million unmarried-partner households, and 605,000 of these were same-sex households. In addition, in 2012, two out of every five opposite-sex unmarried couples lived with at least one biological child of either partner.

Drastic changes in reproduction have had an impact. With the advent of the birth control pill, women could be sexually active and avoid pregnancy. With the loosening of social norms

surrounding parenting and marriage, and the advent of reproductive technologies, men and women can parent without being married, partnered, or even knowing the biological parent
of their offspring.

Additionally, the greater social acceptance of homosexuality and same-sex marriage has led to a blurring of gender
roles in relationships. In couples where both partners are the
same sex, the traditional gender roles can more easily be dis-
carded.

Regardless of opinion on whether or not these changes
have been positive—and authors in this chapter illustrate that
there is disagreement on that issue—it is clear that the changes
of the past few decades have impacted gender roles greatly,
upending the traditional structure. Whether or not these
changes will continue to the point of eliminating gender roles
or whether new roles are created remains to be seen.

> *"Although there is a division of labor in human affairs between the sexes, there are changing social expectations, which are reflected in somewhat different gender roles at different times."*

Changing Gender Roles in Marriage

Fredric Neuman

In the following viewpoint, Fredric Neuman argues that based on what he has seen over the years as a psychiatrist, gender roles in marriage have changed in many ways, but there are still clear gender roles in several areas. Neuman claims that there tends to be a gendered division of labor in marriage that is consistent with past gender roles. Nonetheless, he claims that with respect to finances, religion, parenting, and sex, men and women take on different roles or share responsibility. Neuman is the director of the Anxiety and Phobia Treatment Center at White Plains Hospital in New York.

As you read, consider the following questions:

1. In what way are the household responsibilities not shared equally, in Neuman's opinion?

Fredric Neuman, "Changing Gender Roles in Marriage," *Psychology Today* (blog), January 4, 2013. www.psychologytoday.com/blog/fighting-fear. Copyright © 2013 by Fredric Neuman. All rights reserved. Reproduced by permission.

2. Which sex is most likely to be in charge of family finances now and in the past, according to the author?

3. According to Neuman, which parent is most likely to have the last word in determining child-rearing practices?

Most married couples develop a shared understanding of who does what in their relationship. It is a sometimes unspoken recognition of an inevitable division of labor and responsibilities. The current, commonly agreed, "politically correct" plan for marriage is an equal sharing of chores and other duties; but this plan is not followed now any more than it has been throughout history. In fact, in much of the animal kingdom there is a division of labor which grows inescapably out of different biological imperatives—although here and there in the animal kingdom there are surprising instances of role reversal. Sometimes the male is charged with taking care of the eggs, for instance.

Although there is a division of labor in human affairs between the sexes, there are changing social expectations, which are reflected in somewhat different gender roles at different times. When I grew up, fathers were employed out of the home, and mothers tended to the household. That meant not only housekeeping but taking primary responsibility for child upbringing. Now things are different. Most mothers work. Household responsibilities must be shared. But they are not shared equally. My reading of current expectations in marriage is that men still fix things and take care of the automobiles. Women still have primary responsibility for the proper maintenance of the home and the welfare of the children. If both parents work, for instance, it is more often the mother who takes off time to bring a sick child to the doctor—unless the father's schedule is much more flexible. Most women— although not all—do the cooking and cleaning. Most men—

but not all—do the repairs. Men are likely to assemble the furniture, women are likely to find themselves with the task of cleaning it.

I know that some people, particularly women, are likely to object to these seemingly glib caricatures of the various roles women and men play in marriage—and I am not saying that I think this state of affairs is necessarily the way things *should* be—but I think these generalizations are still a description of how things actually are. With exceptions, of course. None of these general rules applies to every marriage. The following observations are mine alone and may reflect idiosyncrasies of where I live and work. Currently, it seems to me:

The generalizations I made above are more or less true: men take care of mechanical devices: cars, hi-fi systems, appliances and so on. Women tend to be in charge of decorating the house and making other purchases for the home: choosing drapes and carpets, and, of course, making sure they are clean and cared for properly.

Where a couple lives is still more likely to depend on where the husband works, rather than where the woman works. The man is likely to be better paid.

If someone tosses a ball around with the kids, it is likely to be their father. If the kids need to be driven to activities, it is usually the mother who does the driving. She is also likely to be the one buying clothes for them.

Social arrangements, such as dinner with friends, are likely to be managed by the wife. Wives are more likely to initiate discussions about planned vacations.

All sorts of little tasks fall to one or another of a couple almost by chance and habit. The husband might take out the garbage, do the barbecue and carry packages into the house. The wife might dress the children, make arrangements with the handyman, and call family members.

However, there are other tasks which seem to be up for grabs.

Financial Matters

Not long ago, it seemed that husbands were more likely to be in charge of the family finances. Now, I think that either spouse may end up managing the bank account, paying the mortgage and, in general, dealing with a budget—although, often enough, no one is dealing with the budget. It is common now for husbands and wives to have separate checking accounts. Somewhat less common is the practice of some couples of keeping their funds separate. This is especially true if couples are living together, but not yet married.

I am somewhat uncomfortable hearing about such an arrangement. Often I learn about it only when an accusation has been made that someone violated the terms of the agreement, e.g., "I paid the phone bill last month when it was your turn, and I also paid for the hotel rooms, so you should pay a little more of the food bill this month and the dog food." Some of these financial arrangements are very detailed, and it is easy to feel taken advantage of or cheated. The money belongs to both of them in a way, but not in another way. I think there is implicit in such a financial understanding the recognition that there is no real commitment to each other. At least not at that point in time.

It is usually the case that one spouse says "we need this," about a particular expenditure, and the other says, "we can't afford this." Over and over again throughout a marriage, each spouse is likely to take the same position. The person who thinks something—a vacation, a new bathroom—is necessary always thinks what is being considered is necessary, and the other always thinks it is unaffordable. These roles are not gender specific.

Religious Matters

It used to be in some places that women took the religion of their future husbands. There are still places in the world where there are rigid rules about these matters. Some religions will

"I think our relationship is truly gender neutral.

Joseph Giunta, www.CartoonStockcom.

not honor a marriage if it takes place outside the church. Nowadays, in this country, the man's wishes are not determinative. Usually, when there are children, the parent who feels most strongly about religion will get the spouse's consent to bring up the child in that person's religion. More commonly, the children are raised—not very seriously—in both religions or in no religion. It is unusual to find two parents who are prepared to marry who feel equally strongly about their particular religion. In fact, over the years I have encountered fewer people who feel strongly about religion in general. In taking a history, I always ask about religion. More people are not affiliated. Some people say, "I am spiritual," which means that they are not religious.

Child Rearing Practices

No one parent, by virtue of being the mother or the father, has the last word in determining child rearing practices. It can be either; but, usually, one person feels more strongly than the other about discipline and other matters, and that person's opinion is likely to hold sway. Sometimes parents do not come to an understanding about such issues, and ugly confrontations ensue, upsetting the children. Parents who have different attitudes about education are particularly likely to disagree about how much studying a child should do. Children can learn to exploit these differences and become manipulative, which is not in their long-range interest.

Sex

There used to be relatively clear-cut attitudes about sex. The man's wishes were what counted. No one believes that anymore; but there is still an expectation in our culture, that the husband should take the lead in initiating sex. But not all the time. Husbands and wives are not likely to start off automatically in agreement about exactly how much sex they would prefer to have. It is not reasonable to expect that two people will want exactly the same amount of anything, whether it is the number of children they should have, or the number of times they should go on vacations, or the number of times they are required to visit in-laws. These differences can be readily compromised if there is good-will; and the same is true for sexual matters. However, it is true, nevertheless, that often one of a couple (and sometimes both) is unhappy with their sexual adjustment. Usually, the discontent centers on having too little sex; and the person who wants to have more sex is just as likely to be the wife as the husband. Some couples seem to adjust to having very little sex, while other couples do not. The level of dissatisfaction often mirrors other dissatisfactions in the marriage.

Who Is in Charge?

There was a time when husbands were in charge. In some areas of the world that is still plainly the case. In fact, in some distant, but more and more familiar places, like Pakistan or Afghanistan, women are not only cast into a submissive role, but are treated as inferiors. But not in Westchester County in the twenty-first century. In most families here no one would claim to be in charge. Even if someone really thought he/she was in charge, it would be considered bad manners to make such a claim.

Looking over the shoulders of so many families, I find it difficult usually to say if one spouse or another is really in charge. Gender roles are shifting and complicated, as described above. One person can be the final word in one sort of issue, like finances, and have little to say about other matters, such as dealing with the children. Still, there are couples whose friends will agree that one person, or the other, is clearly "the boss." I think this is not necessarily a bad thing. Usually, in these cases it is simply that one person feels more strongly about certain things than the other, or is by temperament more passive than the other. If that person makes most of the decisions in family matters, it does not mean that the other person has a lower status. These roles can change, anyway, in the event of illness or some other family emergency.

The individual and more or less arbitrary division of labor in a marriage is not likely to undermine its success. As is always the case, the success of a marriage will depend primarily on mutual respect and affection.

| "Women have bought into a feminist mystique that has left them more alone and conflicted in their pursuit of fulfillment than ever before."

Feminism Has Harmed Women by Eliminating Natural Gender Roles

Nicole M. Kooistra

In the following viewpoint, Nicole M. Kooistra argues that the last few decades of feminism has harmed women more than helped them. Kooistra claims that the promotion of no-strings-attached sex has prevented or damaged marriages, and she claims that the advice to women to seek work outside the home goes against the innate desires of women and leads to unhappiness. Kooistra, now Nicole M. King, is the managing editor of the Howard Center's quarterly journal, The Family in America: A Journal of Public Policy.

As you read, consider the following questions:

1. What percentage of births in 2011 were to unwed mothers, according to Kooistra?

Nicole M. Kooistra, "Feminism Through the Life Cycle," *The Family in America: A Journal of Public Policy*, vol. 24, no. 4, Winter 2013. Copyright © 2013 by The Howard Center for Family, Religion and Society. All rights reserved. Reproduced by permission.

2. What is the total fertility rate in the United States, as reported by the author?

3. According to Kooistra, inside of most, if not all, women lies what powerful desire?

In the introduction to the Tenth Anniversary Edition of *The Feminine Mystique*, Betty Friedan wrote, "It's frightening when you're starting on a new road that no one has been on before. You don't know how far it's going to take you until you look back and realize how far, how very far you've gone."

Indeed. Forty years after that statement and fifty years after the publication of *The Feminine Mystique*, the road that Friedan embarked upon has led women to places they have never been before—entering the workforce and academia in ever-higher numbers, yes, but also historically low fertility rates, no-fault divorce, and abortion on demand. The emotional consequences for women have not been rosy. [Betsey] Stevenson and [Justin] Wolfers report that, in spite of the fact that all objective measures of women's happiness have risen, both women's subjective well-being and their well-being relative to men have fallen since the 1970s. For the first time in the last 35 years, men report higher levels of happiness than do women.

Friedan's diagnosis of "the problem that has no name"—women's sense of purposelessness—was justified, but her prescriptions have been disastrous. The road that Betty Friedan and second-wave feminists paved has led women to lives new and unfamiliar, but not to a solution to the problem. In following the impact of feminism through three broad categories of the life cycle—education, child-bearing years, and the empty nest—we see that the promises of feminism have fallen flat, as women have bought into a feminist mystique that has left them more alone and conflicted in their pursuit of fulfillment than ever before.

The New Sex-Directed Education

Friedan oft laments what she calls the "sex-directed education" of women. Women, she discovered when interviewing college girls to write her book, embark upon higher education primarily to meet a man and cannot be bothered with academic pursuits. Friedan professes herself to be horrified. When she was in college, she writes, women used to linger outside the classrooms for hours, debating war, marriage, sex, art. Women of 1963 were too occupied painting their nails and keeping dates to bother with the end of Western Civilization. Friedan argues that women have reached this stage because they have been long trained that their primary purpose is sexual. High-school and college curricula have become increasingly "functionalist," oriented toward a woman's sexual function of bearing children.

Friedan's answer is an education that prepares women for a meaningful career outside the home. Women should go to college not for some vague liberal arts degree, but for a degree that sets them on a specific career path. For this to happen, she says, they must learn to explore their sexuality outside of marriage. And although she does not say it, the implicit lesson is that girls must learn that denying their fertility is a necessary step to success.

Women have learned their lesson only too well. We face now a new "sex-directed education," one that explicitly tells young girls that they are sexual beings expected to engage in intercourse before marriage and also expected to protect themselves from the hazards of an unwanted pregnancy. This new sex-directed education is enforced by a variety of the nation's most reputable bodies. The American Academy of Pediatrics recently issued a statement recommending that doctors prescribe emergency contraceptives like Plan B in girls' early teens, before they actually become sexually active. The Centers for Disease Control and Prevention and the American Academy of Pediatrics both recommend that children (boys and girls) receive the HPV [human papillomavirus] vaccine as young as 11 or 12.

The educators are doing their job well, as is seen in current levels of contraception use. The National Center for Health Statistics reports that 61.8% of women ages 15–44 use some form of contraception, and 98% of women who have ever had intercourse have used contraception. Of these, the more educated the woman, the more likely she was to "protect" herself, with daughters of college graduates the most likely to use contraception at first incidence of intercourse (83.9%). Yet in spite of all of this contraception, a staggering 41% of births in 2011 were to unwed mothers. Women have more chemical and mechanical means than ever before to keep themselves from bearing children, and yet, almost half of babies are born outside of wedlock. The implication is clear: Sex and marriage no longer go together, and so, babies and marriage no longer go together, in spite of the fact that research overwhelmingly shows marriage to be the best environment for raising children.

In promoting no-strings-attached sex, this new sex-directed education has both prevented marriages from occurring and damaged the marriages that do occur. A recent study has shown that women who have sex before marriage increase their chances of divorce, and those who have sex before the age of 18 double their odds of a split. Women are being educated to be sexually active before marriage, told that the best way to ensure a career is to postpone marriage and children. To do so, they subject their bodies to one of a number of chemical or surgical procedures, while engaging in behavior that endangers their future marriages. The functionalists may no longer write the curriculum, but we still have a "sex-directed education," one that is far more damaging than any functionalist text ever was.

Seeking Work Outside the Home

Once they reach adulthood, Friedan argues, women of 1963 took pride in checking the box for "occupation: housewife" on the U.S. census. A cult of femininity and motherhood had developed whose design was to keep women in the home. At the same time that women chose "occupation: housewife" as their calling, however, that occupation was becoming less and less fulfilling. Friedan accurately notes the rise of the consumerist household: "Why is it never said that the really crucial function, the really important role that women serve as housewives is *to buy more things for the house.* In all the talk of femininity and woman's role, one forgets that the real business of America is business."

The home was no longer a place where a woman felt useful. The state had taken over the education and care of her children for the majority of most days. Her husband spent all his waking hours in an office or shop miles away. The home did not produce anything. Friedan's solution to the increasing irrelevance of the American home was for women to leave it, just like men did. Seek meaning in a useful vocation, she advised. Hire help to care for the children and do the cleaning.

Women have taken her advice, leaving home and children to the care of others in ever-increasing numbers while searching for more fulfilling lives elsewhere. But those careers, it turns out, are not as meaningful as they had hoped, and most women still cannot squelch that maternal instinct that drives them to *want* to bear and care for children more than anything else in the world. Kay Hymowitz argues in "The Plight of the Alpha Female" that "women are less inclined than men to think that power and status are worth the sacrifice of a close relationship with their children." Women, she says, generally *prefer* being with their children to spending their days in boardrooms and conference calls. Hymowitz reports on a longitudinal study of Booth School of Business graduates at the University of Chicago. The study found that although these new graduates began their careers in equal numbers and earned roughly equal salaries, half of the women had quit in ten years. Ninety percent of the men remained in the workforce. These women, among the best and brightest in the business world and probably well able to afford childcare, chose to leave profitable careers to stay home.

The Desires of Women

Hymowitz also points to some interesting statistics that indicate that women still tend to plan their most intense career-pursuing years around the possibility of having a child. A recent survey of students conducted by University of Wisconsin psychologists showed that most female students were already thinking about ways to cut back their work hours once they became mothers. Similarly, a recent survey of 1,000 mothers conducted by *Forbes* revealed that while only 10% of stay-at-home mothers wished they still worked, about half of working mothers wished they could stay at home. Study upon study has indicated that most women want to have children, and most women who want to have children want to stay home with them or at the very most work part-time. This reality is emphasized by the very few number of what Hymowitz calls female "alphas"—those at the very top of any given career path. Of Fortune 500 company CEOs [chief executive officers], only four percent are women, and Hymowitz argues that this represents women's choice to avoid such careers more than anything else. The same goes for politics—men are still the overwhelming majority in both the Senate and the House.

While the data indicate that women still want to have children and want to stay home with them, however, the stark reality is that fewer women are having fewer children. The mean age of first birth in the U.S. is a bit over 25 years, according to the U.S. Census Bureau, while the preliminary data for 2011 indicates that birth rates for women ages 30–34 are actually higher than birth rates for women ages 20–24. The overall

U.S. birthrate, however, is at an all-time low of 63.2 per 1,000 women, ages 15–44—a total fertility rate of 1.9. Women are either foregoing children or pushing back childbearing until late ages.

What the data do not show is how many of those women would have *liked* to have children after delaying childbirth into their 30s. Recent mathematical models have estimated that by 30, 95% of women have only 12% of their eggs remaining. As later childbirth has become more popular, so have reproductive technologies such as IVF [in vitro fertilization], technologies whose success rate is dubious and whose health impact upon both child and mother are still relatively unknown. Ironically—and sadly—women discover that the high-powered career is not that important to them, while perhaps simultaneously discovering that their fertility is not as buoyant as they had hoped.

The other group in the category of career-minded women are those who manage to have children, but also believe they can "have it all"—in the words of Anne-Marie Slaughter's recent piece in the *Atlantic* that reignited debate over the compatibility of family life and a high-powered career. More women are acknowledging that "having it all" is a delusion, because the lingering reality is that most women still feel a sense of guilt about leaving children for long hours, guilt that men simply do not feel at the same levels. Those women who choose to try to juggle a 60-hour work week with soccer practice, school, and music lessons find themselves torn between two worlds, facing inner conflict that leaves them unsatisfied with their roles. Predictably, those women who do attain the "alpha" jobs are more likely than women in the general population to be childless.

The Problems of Older Women

In interviewing her subjects, Friedan found that many housewives lived in fear of what would happen when the babies

US Women's Lifestyle Preference

If you were free to do either, would you prefer to have a job outside the home, or would you prefer to stay at home and take care of the house and family?

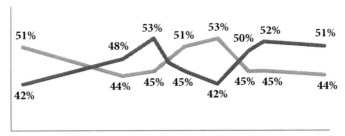

1992 1994 1996 1998 2000 2002 2004 2006 2008 2010 2012

Have a job outside the home

Stay home, take care of house and family

TAKEN FROM: Gallup.

were gone. One purportedly told her that she envied her neighbor, an interior designer: "She knows what she wants to do. I don't know. I never have. When I'm pregnant and the babies are little, I'm *somebody*, finally, a mother. But then, they get older. I can't just keep on having babies."

The contemporary American woman faces perhaps an even starker reality. In 1963, the average woman still had babies. Lots of babies. When she was older, she may still have at least one or two of those children living nearby, and probably a few grandchildren as well. Now, however, with the age of first child rising and the overall birth rate declining, women are increasingly alone in a vulnerable stage of life. With five children, one or two might have stayed close to home. With two, the chances of having a child living nearby dwindle. The children a woman does have are likely postponing their own family as well, denying Mom and Dad both the health and emotional benefits of caretaking.

In addition to being childless, the baby-boomer female is increasingly likely to be divorced. Susan Brown and I-Fen Lin have shown that while the divorce rate for the population at large has remained essentially the same over the past 20 years, divorces have doubled among adults aged 50 and older—so-called "gray divorces." Most of these divorces stem from re-marriages that have fallen apart, as remarriages are much more likely than first marriages to dissolve. What the rise in divorce among this generation means is that all the health, emotional, and economic impacts of a divorce hit women in a stage of life of great transition, when overall health is more likely to be declining. For women in particular, who are much less likely than men to have had a career and consequent sav-ings, the economic impact may be severe.

At the very time of life when a woman should be able to rest and enjoy the fruits and fulfillment of a life well-lived, then, while still being of some use to her family, she finds her-self increasing isolated. If she is like most women, she has not allowed herself to develop a career to the same level as do men, because she wanted to be around for her children when they were growing. The result is that she has not given herself wholeheartedly either to career or to childrearing. Now, in the so-called Golden Years, she has little purpose in life, no com-fort in either work or family.

The Solution for the Future

The problems that Betty Friedan outlined were real. Industri-alization and the consumerism of the 1950s meant that the American household was reduced to little more than a com-fortable hotel, where people slept and perhaps ate a meal or two while conducting their real work elsewhere. Little surprise that women felt stifled and unfulfilled by the role of glorified purchaser. And for Friedan, self-fulfillment was paramount. Women could not be "fulfilled," she believed, unless they held meaningful paid employment. The home was no longer enough to provide fulfillment. But what do these women who have followed Friedan's advice—divorced, childless, grandchildless—have to show for their "self-fulfillment"?

The modern American woman who has tried to follow Friedan's command to pursue a career and raise a family on the side finds herself in constant conflict with her own nature. For inside most if not all women lies a powerful desire to have some children and take care of them. In trying to straddle the worlds of career and homemaker, today's woman finds herself under stress, tired, and, according to most studies, wanting to return home to be with the children. In her later years, she is more likely to be alone and separated from her children and husband. We are no better off today than we were in 1963, and in many ways, we are worse. What, then, is the solution? How are women to be "fulfilled" by the role of wife and mother? The problem lies not in some kind of gender disparity, as Friedan thought, but rather in what [commentator] Wendell Berry calls in *The Unsettling of America* the "sexual division of labor." Labor has always been gendered, Berry argues. Women have tended to focus on the domestic, while men have tended to do the work outside the home. But only with industrialization has the sexual *division* of labor been so pronounced. Men have left the home to work for money, an abstraction, while women have stayed at home doing work that was menial and automated. "Home became," says Berry, "a place for the husband to go when he was not working or amusing himself. It was the place where the wife was held in servitude."

The only way for both sexes to be fulfilled in their work is for work to become human again, for the home to reclaim its authority in American society, and for Americans—men and women—to resume the roles that are rightfully theirs. For that transition to happen, men and women both must make choices that go against the grain. Growing a household garden, homeschooling the children, a small home business, a home office—all these would help. There are signs that we may be moving in the right direction—David Houle's *The Shift Age* argues that Americans are changing the way that they work, foregoing a structured office environment and hierarchical system in which they do not see the end results of their labor for more project-based work that is also more likely to be amenable to flexible hours and home life.

Let us hope that the trend continues. Until the home becomes productive again, we will continue to see the problem that has no name, because women will still lead lives that deny their fundamental human nature and gifts.

"Feminists battled for decades to . . . wrest power from men. Congratulations men, you won."

Feminists Fought Battles and Men Won the War

Brenda Zurita

In the following viewpoint, Brenda Zurita argues that although feminists wanted to achieve equality by changing the culture, they ended up giving more power to men. Zurita claims that by removing the taboo on premarital sex and discouraging male chivalry as sexist, the feminist movement has resulted in a world where men can have sex without commitment and have lost interest in marriage. Zurita is a research fellow for Concerned Women for America's Beverly LaHaye Institute.

As you read, consider the following questions:

1. Zurita claims that women were treated with more respect prior to what cultural event?

2. Zurita cites a survey finding what percentage of women saying they would prefer to pay for their own dinner on a first date?

3. According to the author, a recent study found what difference between the percentage of young women and
the percentage of young men who want to marry?

Feminists battled for decades to change the culture, laws,
and behaviors under the guise of "equality" when, in reality, it was a fight to wrest power from men. Congratulations
men, you won.

Wait, what?

All constraints against men's baser behaviors towards
women have been removed. They are free to have sex with
women without dating, commitment, marriage, or responsibility thanks to feminism.

Before the sexual revolution of the 1960s, women were
treated with more respect. If a man had sex with a woman
and she became pregnant, he was expected to marry her. As
such, pre-marital sex was not as prevalent as it is today.
Women didn't just jump into bed with a man; men had to
court a woman, earn her trust and respect, and then ask for
her hand in marriage. Was there pre-marital sex? Yes, but it
was rarer and held consequences for men.

In today's world, men can sleep around and expect the
woman is on the birth control pill, and if she isn't or it fails,
they expect her to go get an abortion (which is every woman's
right, according to *Roe v. Wade* you know). A third option is
to ignore the possibility altogether, because if she is pregnant,
feminists tell him that it is a woman's choice and it's his fault
as the sperm donor. He has no choice to become a father if
the woman decides she doesn't want to be a mother.

Feminists utilized static analysis when they began down
the path to "empower" women—they would change the rules,
and men would pay for their unjust treatment of women.
However, dynamic analysis would have predicted that women's
easy access to birth control pills and unrestricted abortion
would remove men's responsibility for any consequences of

Marriage Rates for Young Adults

Young adults today are marrying at lower rates and later ages than ever before—only a third (33%) of 18- to 34-year-old women are now married, compared with nearly three quarters (73%) of women this age in 1960. The median age for first marriage is now 27 for women, up from 20 in 1960. And the median age for first-time mothers is now 24, up from 22 in 1960. So while marriage and family still remain among women's top priorities, many are delaying these milestones when compared with earlier generations.

Eileen Patten and Kim Parker, Pew Research Social and Demographic Trends, April 19, 2012.

"free love." Men took advantage of consequence-free sex-on-demand and ended up with more power. Call it what you will—irony, tunnel vision, law of unintended consequences, naiveté.

The steep decline (some say death) of chivalry is another result of the battles. Feminists were offended by men who gave up their seats to women or held the door open for them. Forget about taking a woman out on a date and—gasp!—paying for the date! How demeaning; women can make their own money and pay their own way, thank you very much. A U.K. *Daily Mail* article shows how far we've fallen, concluding that women are suspicious of men who try to help them. One commenter summed it up, "I am not holding this door open because you are a lady, I am holding it open because I am a gentleman."

After the attack on chivalry, dating became the next casualty. A man used to pick up a woman at her residence to go to dinner, a movie, a play, etc., and pay for it, all the while being chivalrous. *The U.K. Telegraph* points to a new survey that shows 82 percent of women would prefer to pay for their dinner on a first date; 78 percent of women would not accept the offer of a man's coat on a cold day; only 8 percent of women said they would accept the offer of a man's seat, and yet, 98 percent said they would like to receive flowers.

As the sexual revolution steam rolled over old-fashioned values, dates faded away until Millennials are left with today's alternatives. A *New York Times* article said, "Instead of dinner-and-a-movie, which seems as obsolete as a rotary phone, they rendezvous over phone texts, Facebook posts, instant messages and other "non-dates" that are leaving a generation confused about how to land a boyfriend or girlfriend." Going on "group dates" or just meeting up at the last minute is typical, as is "hooking up" which entails no-commitment sex.

Feminism told women they could have the same commitment-free sex life they thought men enjoyed. Now men actually are enjoying that, and women are longing for more. To paraphrase an old saying, "Why date a woman when you can get the sex for free?"

It should be no surprise then that men have lost interest in marriage. A Foxnews.com article sheds light on the boomerang effect of feminism's battles: "According to Pew Research Center, the share of women ages eighteen to thirty-four that say having a successful marriage is one of the most important things in their lives rose nine percentage points since 1997—from 28 percent to 37 percent. For men, the opposite occurred. The share voicing this opinion dropped, from 35 percent to 29 percent."

The author asked men why they do not want to marry, and their answer was, "Women aren't women anymore." The article says women today are perceived by men as angry, defensive, and treating men as the enemy.

Feminists pushed the idea that before feminism came to help them, women were powerless. So after the feminist push started in the 1970s to right all wrongs, women are now earning more degrees than men and are the majority of the U.S. workforce. With these advances, women also took on the responsibility for sexual consequences (birth control, abortion, or single-motherhood) and still do the majority of housework and child-rearing when they cohabitate with or marry a man, even when they work full-time, too.

Feminists succeeded in giving men the power to have sex with no commitment or consequence, show no deference to women, save money by not dating, and forgo marriage. Women might have more education and jobs than men now, but they are at the mercy of sexually liberated men who don't want or need to settle down.

Maybe men should send feminists some flowers?

> "Men are caught between an old-fashioned breadwinner ideal and an economic era that no longer delivers the family wage. . . . They can [choose to] feel terrible about themselves, or they can help to change an outdated ideal."

Let's Rethink Masculinity: Real Men Should Be More than Breadwinners

Joan C. Williams

In the following viewpoint, Joan C. Williams argues that although progress has been made from the times in the past when women were deemed inferior and when jobs were strictly gendered, there still exists an ideology of separate spheres. Williams contends that as long as men are expected to live up to norms of conventional masculinity, the movement for gender equality will be thwarted. Williams is the author of Unbending Gender *and a distinguished professor of law at the University of California, Hastings College of Law, in San Francisco.*

As you read, consider the following questions:

1. What percentage of occupations are sex balanced, where men and women are integrated in a rich way, as stated by the author?

2. What gender expectations does Williams identify in support of her view that society still channels separate-spheres ideology?

3. According to Williams, male breadwinner fathers married to homemakers earn how much more money that those in two-job families?

A patient is brought into the emergency room. The surgeon says, "I can't operate on this patient: he's my son." The surgeon is not the patient's father. Why can't the surgeon operate? This classic brainteaser works—and it worked on me—because of the hidden assumption that surgeons are male. The answer: The surgeon is the patient's mother.

The riddle highlights that most jobs are gendered. Only 13 percent of occupations are sex balanced, in the sense of integrating men and women beyond token levels. And most high-paying jobs, blue- as well as white-collar, are associated not only with men but also with masculinity. Thus the personality traits commonly assumed to make for a good engineer or tool-and-die maker (good at technical subjects, not high on people skills) are considered masculine. So are the very different skills assumed to make for a good executive or factory foreman (forceful and assertive, high on people skills).

No logical relationship exists between these two sets of personality traits and skills. Their relationship is historical, based on the high value placed on qualities associated with men and masculinity. Before separate spheres arose in the late 18th century, many women worked as blacksmiths, woodworkers, printers, tinsmiths, brewers, tavern keepers, shopkeepers, shoemakers, barbers and shipwrights. So long as these women were wives acting as "deputy husbands" for men who were away, this seemed appropriate and unobjectionable. Women doing jobs traditionally performed by men did not yet jar sensibilities because men and women were not chiefly defined by their separate spheres.

Women pre-1800 were defined by their inferiority. The premise was that men, as heads of the household, had the right to expect obedience not only from their children but also from their wives. Women needed men's guidance because they were not only physically inferior to men but also intellectually and morally inferior.

The Enlightenment's declaration that all "men" were equal destabilized established notions of women's inferiority. Gradually, women came to be seen as equal, too—in their separate sphere. They went from being seen as morally weak to being considered morally superior. Under separate spheres, the "moral mother" was expected to counterbalance men's pursuit of self-interest in the market sphere, which, still new, was painted as ruthless, "red in tooth and claw."

It turns out that our 21st century common sense faithfully channels separate-spheres ideology. Thus today's typical man is seen as independent, ambitious and competitive, naturally suited to market work and the breadwinner role. Meanwhile, today's typical woman is seen as nurturing, expressive and responsive to the needs of others, naturally suited to homemaking and the emotional work required by secretaries, flight attendants and nurses. These basic tenets of separate spheres continue to shape our default understandings of men and women, reproducing stereotypes that systematically advantage men and disadvantage women in the workplace.

These stereotypes lead to powerful social expectations that link our sense of what one needs to be successful in historically male professions to masculine personality traits and traditionally masculine life patterns. One prominent physicist put it this way: "In particular, our selection procedures tend to select not only for talents that are directly relevant to success in science, but also for assertiveness and single-mindedness." In other words, physicists are expected to have stereotypically masculine personality traits: to be forceful, proactive, assertive—"agentic," to use social psychologists' chosen term.

Physicists, the quote reminds us, are expected to be not only assertive but also single-minded. Hard-driving lawyers, neurosurgeons and investment bankers—indeed, all historically male high-status jobs—also require some version of assertiveness and single-mindedness. In other words, such jobs are designed around masculinity and men.

Masculinity holds the key to understanding why the gender revolution has stalled. As long as men continue to feel threatened by the possibility of being perceived as wimps and wusses unless they live up to the norms of conventional masculinity, we can expect little economic progress for women.

It has been said that masculine norms make American society "an affirmative action plan" for men. Feminists need to be on the front lines of documenting how conventional masculinity disadvantages men as well as women. Consequently, the social regard for stay-at-home fathers is even lower than for stay-at-home mothers. Think of everyday language: When mothers dream about their daughter marrying a "successful" man, most are thinking of paychecks, not Snugli child carriers.

The literature on fatherhood sends a stark message: All fathers are not equal. Breadwinners married to homemakers earn 30 percent more than those in two-job families and encounter favored treatment at work. One study found that fathers were held to lower performance and commitment standards than were men without children, presumably because respondents assumed that since a father "has a family to support," he will work hard. This study reflects the normative father, a breadwinner with a wife who is responsible for children and home. In contrast, a father who discloses that he has family care responsibilities faces job risks. One study found that men are often penalized for taking family leave, especially by other men. Another found that men with even a short work absence due to a family conflict were recommended for fewer rewards and had lower performance ratings.

The choice is clear. Be a manly, successful, ideal worker. Or be a wimpy, nurturing father. This scorn for men seeking to fulfill family responsibilities is commonplace—and unambiguously illegal. Granting parental leave routinely to women but denying it to men is a violation of federal law. So is creating an environment hostile to men who seek parental leave (or, even more bravely, demand flexible work arrangements). Illegal as well is retaliation against men who are courageous enough to ignore the sneers and play an equal role in family caregiving.

A key agenda for modern feminism is to work with men to decrease the penalties encountered by those who flout the expectations that stem from conventional masculinity. When ideal-worker norms police men into breadwinner roles, this hurts not only women. It also hurts many men who cannot live up to the breadwinner ideal. Since most American families cannot live comfortably on one income, many working-class men, as well as many middle-class men, find themselves in the painfully demoralizing position of being unable to "support their families."

Men are caught between an old-fashioned breadwinner ideal and an economic era that no longer delivers the family wage, and are left facing two choices: They can feel terrible about themselves, or they can help to change an outdated ideal. Feminists need to engage men on this issue.

| "Transgender identities challenge us to think about the morphisms of 'sex' and 'gender,' 'woman' and 'man,' 'real' and 'not real.'"

Strict Binary Definitions of Sex and Gender Are Problematic

Patricia J. Williams

In the following viewpoint, Patricia J. Williams argues that the greater visibility of transgendered persons in recent years has led to violence and controversy that illustrate society's discomfort with ambiguity about gender. Williams claims that the debate about transgendered persons shows the inadequacy of a binary gender system and concludes that dealing with the issues surrounding transgendered people create an opportunity to rethink this system. Williams is a professor of law at Columbia University in New York City.

As you read, consider the following questions:

1. What examples does the author give of nonviolent situations that create discomfort for transgendered people?

Patricia J. Williams, "Gender Trouble," *The Nation*, May 23, 2011. Reprinted with permission from the July 22, 2013, issue of The Nation. For subscription information, call 1-800-33-8536. Portions of each week's Nation magazine can be accessed at http://www.thenation.com.

2. Williams cites Smith College's claims that medical discourse still conflates what three distinct conditions that affect sex and gender?

3. Addressing the social ambiguity about transgendered people at single-sex colleges provides an opportunity to master what three lessons, in the author's opinion?

Over the past few years, attacks on transgendered people in public places have been on the rise. In 2009 a transwoman in Queens was pelted with rocks, beer bottles and misogynistic [anti-woman] slurs. Just weeks before in the same borough, two men used a belt buckle to beat a transwoman named Leslie Mora. In late April [2011] a widely disseminated video captured two teenage girls punching and dragging Chrissy Lee Polis from a women's room to the front door of a Baltimore-area McDonald's. That video, made by an employee, shows bystanders just watching, with little move to aid her.

The Challenge of Transgender Identities

Crimes like these often stem from simple homophobia; but they reveal a more specific discomfort with the ambiguity that transgendered people embody. The intensity of that discomfort extends to many situations that fall short of violence. Insults and isolation in housing, the workplace, gyms, schools and always, always in public bathrooms—premised on resolute gender binarism—leave transgendered people forever making the "wrong" choice. There are, for example, queasy debates at Smith [a prestigious women's liberal arts college in Massachusetts] and other women's colleges about how to negotiate the presence of students who are admitted as women but graduate as men.

Transgender identities challenge us to think about the morphisms of "sex" and "gender," "woman" and "man," "real" and "not real." This is a hot topic in academic circles: for example, attempting to disambiguate the notion of "identity" as a matter of legal subjectivity, when, say, a man with a heap of warrants is finally arrested—but by the time the police catch up, he has become a she, and in the name of that transformation asserts as a defense that "he" was a different person. It's easy to dismiss this sort of discussion as funny or unimportant, but I think it's necessary, not merely because it directly affects the lives of the transgendered but because it tests and expands the thinking of those of us who are not transgendered, yet whose collective responses shape the social environment.

Take Smith. Its administration has said it welcomes trans students as part of a diverse community, but apparently not all students and alumnae agree. For some, a commitment to remaining a women's college rests on assumptions about what a woman is as a biological matter, what gender is as a social construction and why a woman's experience is, or is deemed to be, different from that of a man. Trans students evoke squeamishness particularly among older alums, as well as among those who come to a "single sex" school for its white-glove, ladylike connotations, or perhaps out of commitment to women's education as a form of empowerment ([feminist icon] Gloria Steinem went to Smith, after all). This contentious conversation scrutinizes not just the gender of individual students but overall institutional identity. The debate at Smith brought to the fore, for example, those who were unhappy to see their school's feminine image newly shared with transmen.

The debate is difficult precisely because it feels so new— and in some ways it is. Sex reassignment technologies are so novel that the accompanying medical discourse still conflates those who have ambiguous genitalia; those whose endocrine systems are ambiguously skewed; and those whose psychology is felt to be at odds with their biology. And what about the culture of elective cosmetic surgery, or the cult of physical perfection that drives even normatively gendered people to feel "not normative enough" and so seek to become "more feminine" or "more masculine" through the wizardry of nose jobs, labial stitching, liposuction, pectoral implants and breast enhancement?

The Categories of Sex and Gender

So what do we mean when we ask a pregnant person if "it" is a boy or a girl? The inquiry seems permissible only *in utero*. We get edgy when we don't already know the answer when encountering a full-grown adult. Do we expand our meaning so that "woman" includes those who may have been born with uncertain genitalia but who grew up being dressed, viewed, identified as female from birth? Do we include that category of people who regarded themselves as men from the very beginning of childhood consciousness yet who, in asserting that sense of self, are not privileged with the perquisites of (white, straight) masculinity but are instead branded as freaks or frauds?

Most difficult of all, what might it mean to explode the entire category of "woman" as anything like a stable designation? What does that mean for the status of women's colleges, women's sports, to say nothing of the proverbial ladies' room? After all, it's not as though men have never been on the campuses of women's colleges. I went to a women's college, and "gentlemen callers" were everywhere—at meals, in seminars, in bedrooms and bathrooms, all but climbing in the windows on weekends. But those were "men" defined in a clear, binary and thoroughly heterosexual context.

To engage in gender-bending means that we are thrown into confusion with regard to everything from Title IX to the college rankings of *U.S. News & World Report*. Rightly or wrongly, women's and men's identities are still largely linked to the preservation of images of good wives in pearls and husbands in spats or, as one of the teenagers in the McDonald's assault put it, to literally beating back competition for the affections of "my man" (or "woman," as the case may be).

There are lessons to be mastered in all this, about principles of antidiscrimination and freedom of expression; about the complexities of perceived reputation ("I don't want to be sneered at for still having a woman's body," said a Bryn Mawr [prestigious Pennsylvania women's liberal arts college] student in the process of changing genders); and about institutional investments, dependent as they are on assessments of risk (Smith's endowment managers are no doubt sweating bullets, given the power of alums as donors). Resolving these conflicts with dignity and thoughtfulness is no less important than educating and prosecuting those who use sticks and stones to beat away their terror of humanity's infinite variability.

Periodical and Internet Sources Bibliography

The following articles have been selected to supplement the diverse views presented in this chapter.

Noah Berlatsky	"When Men Experience Sexism," *The Atlantic*, May 29, 2013.
Adam Carolla	"Women, Hear Me Roar," Townhall, December 24, 2010. www.townhall.com.
Tracy Clark-Flory	"Why Are Men Still Proposing?," *Salon*, May 12, 2013. www.salon.com.
Alexis Coe	"'Don't Ask, Don't Get': How to Fix the Gender Gap in Salary Negotiations," *The Atlantic*, January 10, 2013.
Richard Dorment	"Why Men Still Can't Have It All," *Esquire*, June–July 2013.
Peggy Drexler	"Why Aren't Women Voting for Women?," *Psychology Today*, January 4, 2013.
Michelle Goldberg	"Why (Some) Men Still Have It All," *Democracy Journal*, Fall 2012.
Amanda Hess	"The US Has One of the Worst Science Gender Gaps in the Developed World," *Slate*, February 8, 2013. www.slate.com.
Melissa Kirk	"In Defense of Men," *Psychology Today*, October 3, 2012.
Amanda Marcotte	"Mad 21st Century Men," *American Prospect*, March 26, 2012.
Christina Hoff Sommers, interviewed by Kathryn Jean Lopez	"What About Our Boys?," *National Review*, September 16, 2013.

For Further Discussion

Chapter 1

1. Rebecca Solnit argues that same-sex couples should be allowed to marry in order to promote equality, whereas Andreas J. Köstenberger believes same-sex marriage defies the natural purpose of marriage. For the purpose of making a case for legal marriage, does it matter that Köstenberger's argument is based on the biblical definition of marriage? Why or why not?

2. Mackubin Thomas Owens gives three reasons to oppose allowing women in combat positions in the military. Does William Saletan's response to this viewpoint successfully respond to each of these three reasons? Why or why not?

Chapter 2

1. Jessica Valenti argues that society assumes that all women want to be mothers, and Matt Villano argues that society assumes all men are not good at parenting. Are these two assumptions contradictory or compatible? Explain your answer.

2. Laurie Shrage argues that men do not have as much reproductive autonomy as women. Write a response to Shrage, arguing that men's not having as much reproductive autonomy is not a problem.

Chapter 3

1. In this chapter, several of the authors discuss whether discrimination affects the treatment of women in the workplace. Identify a specific point of disagreement between at least two of the authors, noting the facts each author adduces in support of his or her viewpoint.

2. Since the ability to get pregnant is a real physical difference between men and women, should special accommodations be made for women in the workplace? Backing up your view with quotes from at least one of the viewpoints from this chapter, explain why or why not.

Chapter 4

1. Nicole M. Kooistra argues that feminism has made women's lives harder. Does the viewpoint by Fredric Neuman disprove or support her arguments, in your opinion? Cite specific examples from both viewpoints in explaining your answer.

2. Patricia J. Williams discusses society's discomfort with ambiguity about gender and suggests that a too-strict binary definition of sex and gender is to blame. What are the alternatives to a binary definition? Suggest at least two.

Organizations to Contact

*The editors have compiled the following list of organizations
concerned with the issues debated in this book. The descriptions
are derived from materials provided by the organizations. All
have publications or information available for interested readers.
The list was compiled on the date of publication of the present
volume; the information provided here may change. Be aware
that many organizations take several weeks or longer to respond
to inquiries, so allow as much time as possible.*

Concerned Women for America (CWA)

1015 Fifteenth St. NW, Ste. 1100, Washington, DC 20005
(202) 488-7000 • fax: (202) 488-0806
e-mail: mail@cwfa.org
website: www.cwfa.org

Concerned Women for America is a public policy women's organization that has the goal of bringing biblical principles into
all levels of public policy making. The CWA focuses its promotion of biblical values on six core issues—family, the sanctity of human life, education, pornography, religious liberty,
and national sovereignty—using the avenues of prayer, education, and social influence. Among the organization's brochures,
fact sheets, and articles available on its website is "Vacation
Surprise: Men Allowed in Women's Restrooms."

Equal Rights Advocates (ERA)

180 Howard St., Ste. 300, San Francisco, CA 94105
(415) 621-0672 • fax: (415) 621-6744
e-mail: info@equalrights.org
website: www.equalrights.org

Equal Rights Advocates is a national civil rights organization
dedicated to protecting and expanding economic and educational access and opportunities for women and girls. It advocates for women's equality through public education, legisla-

tive lobbying, and litigation. The ERA publishes several reports and fact sheets, including the Know Your Rights brochure *Sex Harassment at Work.*"

Families and Work Institute (FWI)
267 Fifth Ave., 2nd Fl., New York, NY   10016
(212) 465-2044 • fax: (212) 465-8637
e-mail: publications@familiesandwork.org
website: www.familiesandwork.org

The Families and Work Institute is a nonprofit, nonpartisan research organization that studies the changing workforce, family, and community. It aims to find research-based strategies that benefit American employers and employees, their families, their communities, and the institutions that support them. The FWI publishes the ongoing studies National Study of the Changing Workforce and National Study of Employers, as well as numerous reports on its research.

Family Research Council (FRC)
801 G St. NW, Washington, DC   20001
(202) 393-2100 • fax: (202) 393-2134
website: www.frc.org

The Family Research Council is an organization dedicated to the promotion of traditional ideas of marriage and family and of the sanctity of human life in national policy. The FRC's team of policy experts reviews data and analyzes proposals that impact family law and policy making in the federal government's legislative and executive branches, as well as filing amicus briefs in relevant court cases. The FRC publishes several brochures and other publications, including "The Defense of Marriage Act: What It Does and Why It Is Vital for Traditional Marriage in America."

Fawcett Society
1–3 Berry St., London   EC1V 0AA
   United Kingdom
+44 (0)207 253 2598

e-mail: info@fawcettsociety.org.uk
website: www.fawcettsociety.org.uk

The Fawcett Society campaigns for women's equality and rights at home, at work, and in public life. The society uses independent research and evidence to better understand key issues and to generate media coverage, reports, and briefings that both increase awareness and put pressure on powerful decision makers to act. The Fawcett Society publishes a twice-yearly magazine, *StopGap*, and a monthly e-bulletin.

Gender Spectrum
1271 Washington Ave. #834, San Leandro, CA   94577
(510) 567-3977
e-mail: info@genderspectrum.org
website: www.genderspectrum.org

Gender Spectrum provides education, training, and support for the creation of a gender-sensitive and inclusive environment for all children and teens. Gender Spectrum provides consultation, training, and events designed to help families, educators, professionals, and organizations understand and address the concepts of gender identity and expression. Gender Spectrum publishes several resources that are available on its website, including "Understanding Gender."

The Howard Center
934 N. Main St., Rockford, IL   61103
(815) 964-5819 • fax: (815) 965-1826
e-mail: info@profam.org
website: www.profam.org

The Howard Center is a nonprofit research center that aims to demonstrate and affirm family and religion as the foundation of a virtuous and free society. Along with the World Congress of Families, its international network, the Howard Center aims to promote lifelong marriage for one man and one woman, believing that marriage is the fundamental social unit essential to a good society. The Howard Center publishes the quarterly journal *The Family in America*.

Human Rights Campaign (HRC)

1640 Rhode Island Ave. NW, Washington, DC   20036-3278
(202) 628-4160 • fax: (202) 347-5323
e-mail: hrc@hrc.org
website: www.hrc.org

The Human Rights Campaign is America's largest civil rights organization working to achieve lesbian, gay, bisexual, and transgender (LGBT) equality. The HRC works to secure equal rights for LGBT individuals at the federal and state levels by lobbying elected officials and mobilizing grassroots supporters. Among the organization's publications is the report "Transgender Visibility Guide."

National Coalition for Men (NCFM)

932 C St., Ste. B, San Diego, CA   92101
(888) 223-1280
e-mail: ncfm@ncfm.org
website: www.ncfm.org

The National Coalition for Men is a nonprofit educational organization that aims to raise awareness about the ways sex discrimination affects men and boys. It uses activism through its many chapters to end sex discrimination. The NCFM publishes *Transitions: Journal of Men's Perspectives*.

National Organization for Men Against Sexism (NOMAS)

3500 E. Seventeenth Ave., Denver, CO   80206
(720) 466-3882
e-mail: info@nomas.org
website: www.nomas.org

NOMAS is an activist organization of men and women supporting positive changes for men. It advocates a perspective that is pro-feminist, gay affirmative, antiracist; is dedicated to enhancing men's lives; and is committed to justice on a broad range of social issues, including class, age, religion, and physical abilities. NOMAS's website contains news, articles, and position statements, including "Position Statement on Homophobia."

National Organization for Women (NOW)

1100 H St. NW, 3rd fl., Washington, DC   20005
(202) 628-8669 • fax: (202) 785-8576
website: www.now.org

NOW is the largest organization of feminist activists in the United States and works to bring about equality for all women by eliminating discrimination and harassment in the workplace, schools, the justice system, and all other sectors of society; securing abortion, birth control, and reproductive rights for all women; ending all forms of violence against women; eradicating racism, sexism, and homophobia; and promoting equality and justice in American society. NOW has many publications available at its website, including the fact sheet "Women Deserve Equal Pay."

National Parents Organization

PO Box 270760, Boston, MA   02127-0760
(617) 542-9300
e-mail: parents@nationalparentsorganization.org
website: www.nationalparentsorganization.org

The National Parents Organization is a charitable and educational organization focused on promoting shared parenting, where both parents have equal standing raising children after a separation or divorce. The organization aims to reform the family courts to treat fathers and mothers as equally important to the well-being of their children, to make shared parenting after separation or divorce the norm, and to arrange finances after separation or divorce equitably. The National Parents Organization publishes a weekly newsletter and posts articles on its website.

Bibliography of Books

Katrina Alcorn   *Maxed Out: American Moms on the Brink*. Berkeley, CA: Seal, 2013.

Barbara J. Berg   *Sexism in America: Alive, Well, and Ruining Our Future*. Chicago: Lawrence Hill, 2009.

Francine D. Blau, Marianne A. Ferber, and Anne E. Winkler   *The Economics of Women, Men, and Work*. Boston: Prentice Hall, 2010.

Kate Bornstein and S. Bear Bergman, eds.   *Gender Outlaws: The Next Generation*. Berkeley, CA: Seal, 2010.

Susan J. Carroll and Richard L. Fox   *Gender and Elections: Shaping the Future of American Politics*. New York: Cambridge University Press, 2010.

Susan S. Chuang   *Gender Roles in Immigrant Families*. New York: Springer, 2013.

Lori Duron, Neil Patrick Harris, and David Burtka   *Raising My Rainbow: Adventures in Raising a Fabulous, Gender Creative Son*. New York: Broadway, 2013.

Cordelia Fine   *Delusions of Gender: How Our Minds, Society, and Neurosexism Create Difference*. New York: Norton, 2010.

Jeanne Flavin   *Our Bodies, Our Crimes: The Policing of Women's Reproduction in America*. New York: New York University Press, 2009.

Guy Garcia	*The Decline of Men: How the American Male Is Tuning Out, Giving Up, and Flipping Off His Future.* New York: HarperCollins, 2009.
Kay S. Hymowitz	*Manning Up: How the Rise of Women Has Turned Men into Boys.* New York: Basic Books, 2011.
Dafna Lemish	*Screening Gender on Children's Television: The Views of Producers Around the World.* New York: Routledge, 2010.
Hilary Lips	*Sex and Gender: An Introduction.* Boston: McGraw-Hill/Higher Education, 2008.
Dorothy E. McBride and Janine A. Parry	*Women's Rights in the USA: Policy Debates and Gender Roles.* New York: Routledge, 2011.
Liza Mundy	*The Richer Sex: How the New Majority of Female Breadwinners Is Transforming Sex, Love, and Family.* New York: Simon and Schuster, 2012.
June E. O'Neill and Dave M. O'Neill	*The Declining Importance of Race and Gender in the Labor Market: The Role of Employment Discrimination Policies.* Washington, DC: AEI Press, 2012.
Katherine J. Parkin	*Food Is Love: Food Advertising and Gender Roles in Modern America.* Philadelphia: University of Pennsylvania Press, 2006.

Hanna Rosin	*The End of Men: And the Rise of Women*. New York: Riverhead Books, 2012.
Paula S. Rothenberg, ed.	*Race, Class, and Gender in the United States: An Integrated Study*. New York: Worth, 2010.
Alena Amato Ruggerio	*Media Depictions of Brides, Wives, and Mothers*. Lanham, MD: Lexington, 2012.
Robyn Ryle	*Questioning Gender: A Sociological Exploration*. Thousand Oaks, CA: Pine Forge Press, 2012.
Peggy Reeves Sanday	*Female Power and Male Dominance: On the Origins of Sexual Inequality*. Cambridge: Cambridge University Press, 1994.
Sheryl Sandberg	*Lean In: Women, Work, and the Will to Lead*. New York: Knopf, 2013.
Julia Serano	*Excluded: Making Feminist and Queer Movements More Inclusive*. Berkeley, CA: Seal, 2013.
Christina Hoff Sommers	*The War Against Boys: How Misguided Policies Are Harming Our Young Men*. New York: Simon and Schuster, 2013.
Matt Bernstein Sycamore	*Nobody Passes: Rejecting the Rules of Gender and Conformity*. Berkeley, CA: Seal, 2007.

Index